Nature's Art Box

Nature's

From t-shirts to twig baskets, **65 cool projects** for crafty kids

Art

to **make with natural materials** you can find anywhere.

Box

Written by
Laura C. Martin
with drawings by
David Cain

Storey Publishing

The mission of Storey Publishing is to serve our customers by
publishing practical information that encourages
personal independence in harmony with the environment.

Edited by Karen Levy and Deborah Burns
Designed by Wendy Palitz and Susan Bernier
Cover art by Laura Martin
Indexed by Eileen Clawson

The information in this book is true and complete to the best of our knowledge.
All recommendations are made without guarantee on the part of the author or
Storey Publishing. The author and publisher disclaim any liability in connection
with the use of this information. For additional information, please contact
Storey Publishing, 210 MASS MoCA Way, North Adams, MA 01247.

Storey books are available for special premium and promotional uses
and for customized editions. For further information, please call
800-793-9396.

Printed in China by R.R. Donnelley
10 9 8

Library of Congress Cataloging-in-Publication Data

Martin, Laura C.
  Nature's art box / Laura C. Martin.
      p. cm.
  Summary: Presents more than sixty projects made from natural materials that are
  available almost anywhere.
  Includes bibliographical references and index.
  ISBN 978-1-58017-503-6 (hardcover: alk. paper)
  ISBN 978-1-58017-490-9 (pbk.: alk. paper)
  1. Nature craft—Juvenile literature. [1. Nature craft. 2. Handicraft.] I. Title.
TT160.M2643 2003
745.5—dc21   2002154374

Dedication

To my goddaughter, Caitlin Coogle, with love.

Acknowledgments

This book is a happy union of the two loves of my life — art and nature. My scientific training was acquired at the University of Georgia; my artistic training came, primarily, from the New York Botanical Garden. I am grateful for the teachers and friends I met at each place and I salute their knowledge and skills.

But without my family, this book would not have been possible. It is a large and diverse family, passionate about art and dedicated to the preservation of the earth. In particular, I would like to thank my daughter, Cameron, whose ideas, artistic knowledge, and enthusiasm are invaluable to me; my son, Dave, whose lifelong dedication to the conservation of the earth is, and always has been, a great inspiration to me; my father, Ken Coogle, who, after 96 years, still manages to make magic out of wood with his turned bowls; and my mother, Lois Coogle, who, after 87 years, still believes that every day should be filled with art and laughter.

Contents

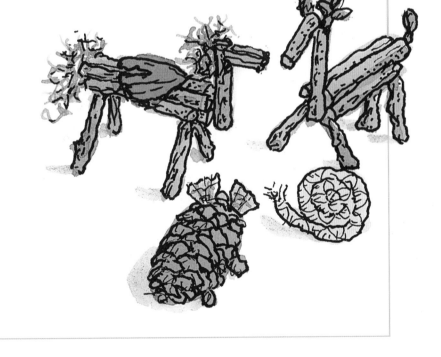

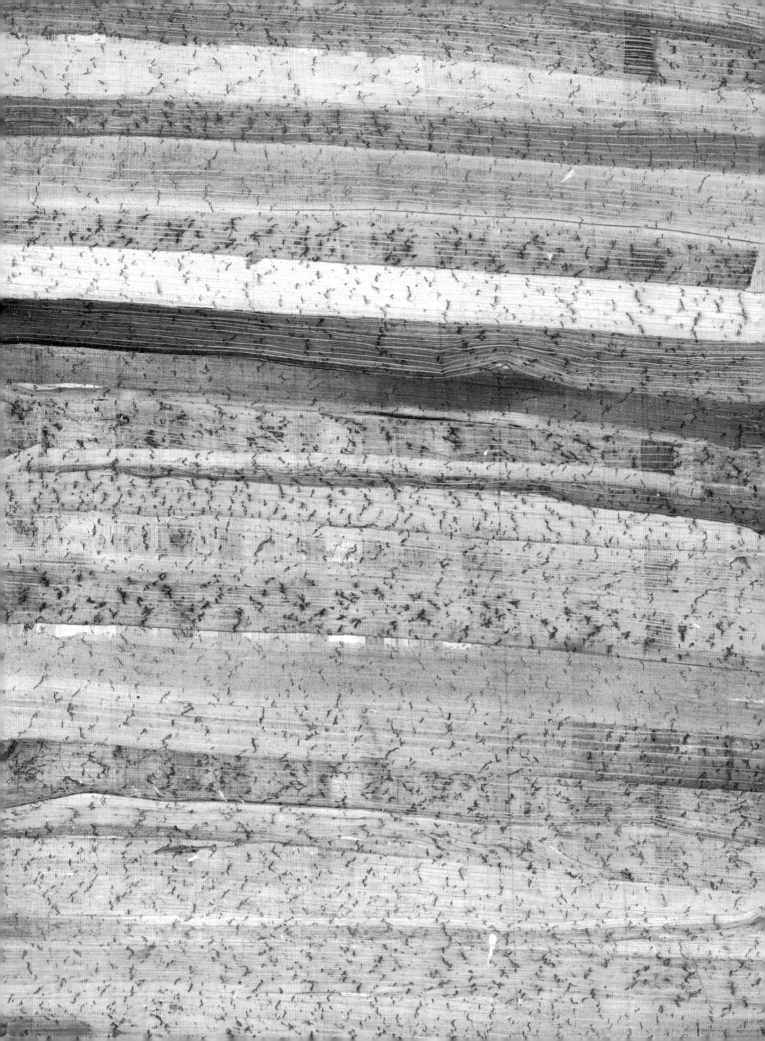

Part One

Art From Nature

The Gifts of the Earth

What do you picture when you think of making crafts? Plastic canvas and Popsicle sticks? Think again! To **craft** means to make something with your hands, and people have been making crafts since time began. In ancient times, people did not have stores that sold craft supplies, so they had to use whatever they could find.

You can do this, too. Once you begin to look around, you'll be amazed at how many things can be created just from objects you find in nature. What's more, when you use natural materials for crafts the results are always beautiful.

Peek inside the art box that nature has given us and you'll see that there is beauty in every nook and cranny of our world. All you have to do is open your eyes and look. One way to truly see the beauty of the earth is to look with the eyes of an artist, for artists learn to really *see* something rather than just glance at it.

Nature has colors and patterns that no artist could ever draw or paint nearly as well. They are the gifts of the earth. But we can work hand in hand with nature and use the gifts she has given us to create things that are touched with her beauty.

An Ax as Art?

The idea is not a new one. Since the beginning of time, people have used the treasures of the earth to make what they need. Using plants, animals, stones, clay, and trees, they fed themselves, made clothes, and built shelters. And then, when time and inspiration allowed, they made those useful items beautiful as well.

Take, for example, a hand ax made in South Africa more than 600,000 years ago. Hand axes were some of the first tools made by humans. They were simple pieces of stone that had been chipped with other stones to make two sharp edges. They were used to cut through meat and bones and to slice through animal skins. But archaeologists have discovered a few special and very beautiful hand axes that were never used. Scientists guess that those were given as gifts to a chief and were meant to be looked at and admired. In other words, they were pieces of art.

Tools remained primitive for hundreds of thousands of years. But some 32,000 years ago, humans were creating art, and in particular, paintings on cave walls.

The First Paintings

The most famous cave paintings are in the Lascaux Cave in southern France. The figures on the cave walls, mainly animals, are painted in red, black, and yellow. They vary in size from forms larger than life to a horse no more than a hand width high. They are found deep in the caves, where it is dark and difficult to get to. The artists may have stood on scaffolds or supports so they could reach the highest points on the cave walls.

Why did artists paint on cave walls? What made them travel deep into a dark cave to paint pictures of animals and half-humans? We will never be absolutely sure of the answers to these questions, but we can make some guesses. The location of the art suggests that it was somehow associated with ceremonies and rituals. Maybe these were healing ceremonies, or connected to prayers for a good hunt.

CAVE PAINTINGS

The Lascaux Cave paintings were found in 1940 by four boys who were searching for buried treasure. While walking through the woods, they came across a partially uprooted tree. They started digging and kept at it until the opening was big enough for them to slide down, feet first. They had only a homemade kerosene lamp to guide them, but when they shined the light on the wall of the cave, they were amazed at the paintings they saw.

The boys returned the next day with a brighter lantern so they could see better. By the third day they were charging a few cents to other children who wanted to visit the cave — no adults were allowed. But that little business venture didn't last long; when word of the cave spread, the family who owned the land developed it into a tourist attraction. They put in electric lights and made steps going down to the cave, and thousands of people came to see the ancient paintings. Unfortunately, the lights and changes in air began to destroy the paintings, so in 1963 the caves were closed to the public.

Who can guess what would have happened if the boys had kept it "children only"? What would you have done if you had discovered this cave?

It wasn't until about 1,000 years ago that the tribes from the southwestern United States left their own artistic marks on the rocks and caves near their homeland. We can still see them today at national parks such as Canyonlands and Arches in Utah. There are many, many animal figures painted on the rocks. There are few human figures, but there are lots of hands, which were painted in all sizes. Some people believe this rock art was ceremonial as well, for Native Americans believe that all things in nature, particularly animals, are spiritual.

Native Americans from all tribes shared, and still do, some of the same beliefs, mainly a deep reverence for the natural environment. They understood that the gifts from the earth were limited and could eventually run out. Their most important ceremonies were prayers of thanksgiving to the earth and respectful requests that the gifts of nature be replenished.

LOOK WITH THE EYES OF AN ARTIST

Try looking at a simple object with the eyes of an artist. Let's start with a pinecone. You have probably seen dozens, if not hundreds, of pinecones. Pick up one and really look at it. Look at the way it is put together. Look at the tiny tips at the end of each piece. Are they prickly or smooth? Are they shiny or dull? Try to pull the pinecone apart — it's probably harder than you thought! Not only is it beautiful, but it's strong, too. Until you stop to really examine the treasures of nature, you'll never know how incredible they are.

We Still Need Nature

Today, we are still dependent on nature. Every day we must use some of the earth's treasures for our very existence. Most of our homes are built of bricks or wood, both of which come from nature. We use water from lakes and streams, and we rely on nature for almost all the food we eat. If flowers disappeared from the earth, humans would become extinct (almost all the foods we eat either come from flowering plants or depend on those plants); but if humans disappeared from the earth, the flowers would get along just fine.

We depend on nature for more than our mere existence. We also rely on her for beauty. What a dull and dreary place this earth would be without the exquisite variety of nature all around us. Our appreciation of beauty makes us uniquely human. Other animals must have food, water, and shelter, too, but it is only humans who find joy in the beauty of the earth.

The challenge of this book is not to see how many things you can make from what you find in nature. You can make hundreds — it's not difficult. The real quest is for you to stop and really look at nature with new eyes. Yes, you'll make some things that are so beautiful you'll want to keep them forever, but what is even better is that you'll begin to look at the world around you in a different way, and appreciate it in ways you never have before.

Nature is abundant in her generosity, but we must learn to use her treasures wisely. I hope that as you discover the beauty of these natural gifts, you will also discover a deeper love for the earth. I hope you will learn to be a partner with nature so that our planet will continue to grow and bloom for many generations to come.

Getting Started

Whether you live in a cabin in the woods, a house in the suburbs, or an apartment in the city, you'll find natural treasures that you can turn into a huge number of projects and gifts. Fortunately, most of these treasures are free. They are the gifts from the earth, so use them wisely. Sometimes you may have to purchase some items from a craft store, but they will be pretty inexpensive. Happily for artists, many craft stores sell shells, pinecones, and moss.

When you pick up items from the out-of-doors, do so carefully, always aware of your responsibility to conserve. Think about the future. If you pick all the flowers from a field, what will others use and, more important, how will seeds develop for next year's flowers? If you pick up all the nuts and pinecones, how will new trees grow and what will the squirrels eat? Be aware that nature's treasures are limited and only nature herself can replenish them. Gather treasures carefully and wisely, leaving more for other artists and for the birds and animals that share our earth.

To help you find natural treasures, this book has a section called **Nature Skills** (see pages 200–211). It contains descriptions of many of the natural items you can use for our projects. These are only suggestions. You will use what is available to you. If you are not certain of the identification of a certain plant, though, be sure you ask someone before you pick it. Some plants cause itching or are poisonous.

The Nature Skills section also answers basic questions about some flowers, ferns, trees, and shells you may find. You will find answers to such questions as, What does it look like? Where can I find it, and when? How can I use it?

What Can You Use?

Almost anything you find in nature can be used for *something*. Some items will be more useful than others, and some areas of the country will have more to offer. The challenge is to be creative in coming up with uses for what you have. For example, in this book you'll find directions for making a little canoe out of an okra pod. **Okra** (see pages 62–63) is a vegetable that grows particularly well in the South. If you don't happen to have okra pods, substitute what you do have — whatever is in the basic shape of a canoe, such as a curved stick or a milkweed pod.

Gourds are sometimes difficult to find or to grow, but you can buy them at a craft store or through an Internet Web site. If you can't find them, however, call on your imagination. For example, perhaps a large **nut** or **seedpod** would work just as well. Use this book for inspiration and ideas, but create your art yourself, using the many natural materials available to you.

Many of the projects call for **moss** and **lichen**. Although you can find these growing in most areas of the country, it is better to purchase sheet moss, Spanish moss, and lichen from a craft store than to dig up live moss and lichen from the woods.

A few projects suggest using **bark**. Everyone knows that bark grows on trees — but don't take it off a living tree! Don't do anything that may harm or scar the natural world. Instead, look around in the woods or even in your neighborhood and find a tree limb that has fallen, and pull some bark off that.

Cornhusks are found on fresh corn, of course, but the best husks for crafts come from field corn (corn grown especially to feed cattle), not eating corn. You can purchase husks from a craft store or from a supermarket that sells them for making Mexican tamales.

As you search for natural treasures, you'll become more aware of the passage of the seasons and of the gifts that come with the different times of year. Not only will you become more aware of the seasons, but you'll also become better acquainted with the wild and wonderful places near your home, whether they are in a park or in your own backyard. Consider keeping a journal. In it you can record the success of your projects and make notes about the best places to find pinecones, acorns, dried grasses, and other treasures.

Not-from-Nature Materials

Although ancient artisans had to find everything they used from nature to create their art, we have the advantage of human-made materials that make crafting much, much easier. For example, glue was first used 5,000 years ago to make furniture in Egypt. The glue was originally made from the hides and bones of animals or from fish. Luckily, there are many kinds of glues we can buy today, making our crafting much easier.

One of the easiest glues to use comes in the form of a **glue stick**, which looks like a fat pen and leaves a strip of glue wherever you put it. This is excellent for working with paper. Some glue sticks are made for use on fabrics as well. **Craft glue**, such as Sobo, is good for projects using cloth or leather. It costs more than regular "school glue," but it works much better. There are many other types of glue, including "designer" **tacky glue** and **E6000**; both are great adhesives but can be tricky to work with. Experiment with them and choose the ones that are the least expensive, the easiest to use, and work the best for your particular project.

The fastest way to glue something is with a **hot glue gun** and **glue sticks**. A hot glue gun is a little device with a trigger that feeds the glue stick through it, heats it up, and then drops hot liquid glue. Soon after the glue is exposed to air, it dries. It can be a magical tool, because you can glue things almost immediately, but it can also hurt if you put your fingers on the hot glue. Always get adult permission and supervision before you start.

RULES FOR PICKING

- **BE COURTEOUS.** Unless a plant is growing in your own yard or garden, don't pick it without first receiving permission.

- **BE CAREFUL.** There are poisonous plants growing throughout North America. Know what you are picking before you touch anything. If you're not sure, ask a knowledgeable adult.

- **BE THOUGHTFUL.** Don't pick more than you will need for your art project. Leave lots of plants for animals, insects, and birds, as well as for other people — to use or just to enjoy.

GLUE GUN CAUTION!

Be careful when you use a hot glue gun. Always follow the directions on the package and get adult permission and supervision before you start. It's easy to burn yourself with hot glue, but remember this one rule: *If you don't touch the glue, it won't burn you.* **It sounds simple, but you'll be amazed at how many times you get carried away and stick your fingers right onto the hot glue. Use a long skewer instead of your finger to push materials with glue on them. If you rub cooking oil onto the skewer first, it will not stick to the glue as much.**

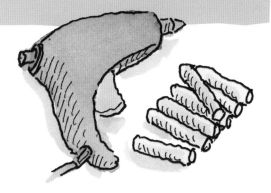

"Cool melt" glue guns are available but are best used with simple materials, such as paper. Try one, though — you may find that it's a good substitute for the hot glue.

Adhesive tape (such as Scotch tape) is also helpful. For some of the projects, you'll want tape that's removable, so you can use it on paper and then take it off when you're through with your project without tearing the paper. Double-sided tape is good for many projects, particularly those that use paper.

Of course, there are ways to get things to stick together without using paste or glue. Since the beginning of time, people have used pieces of leather or hide and strong vines to lash things together. In the crafts world, **raffia** is great for tying things together. Raffia, which is made from a palm tree, looks like long, skinny corn-husks. Because it's a natural material, it looks great on nature crafts. Use it to tie things together, to make bows, and for weaving, for example. You can also use **string**, of course, and if you've dyed it yourself, it will look very good. Plastic **twistie ties**, those little pieces of covered wire that come with plastic bags, are great to have around when things just won't stay together any other way. They are very helpful for small wreaths that want to fly apart. **Leather laces**, even boot-laces, are useful, too. They are natural — and strong.

Sewing is another way to keep things together. If you know how to work a sewing machine, this is definitely the fastest way to stitch, but the projects in this book require so little sewing that it can easily be done by hand. Needles come in many sizes with different-sized eyes (holes). A regular sewing needle is fine for stitching fabric. If you want to use clear fishing line, yarn, or string, you'll need a larger needle with a larger eye, such as an embroidery needle.

Clay is a wonderful material for building crafts. It is easily formed and can give you a great base for things that would otherwise not stand by themselves. Although making clay from dirt and shaping it into pots is an art in itself (see pages 79–80), store-bought clay is quick and easy to use for building purposes.

Colorful **paint** can make a craft look special. There are many kinds, including poster paints, tempera, acrylics, fabric paints, oils, craft paints, and watercolors.

Making Your Own Paste and Glue

Why not make your own paste and glue? Paste should be used mostly for paper crafts; you'll need glue for projects involving fabric, leather, and paper. (This project requires adult supervision.)

For paste you will need:

small bowl

mixing spoon

½ cup whole wheat or white flour

water (about ⅓ cup)

small pan

stovetop or electric burner

airtight plastic container

How to do it:

1 In the bowl, mix the wheat or white flour with enough water to make a liquid paste that looks something like cake batter. Mix well so there are no lumps.

2 Pour the mixture into the pan on the stove and turn the heat to medium. Heat, stirring gently, until it comes to a boil. Remove from the heat immediately. Cool. Store in an airtight container.

3 Check the texture of the paste when you're ready to use it. If it's too hard, add a drop or two of warm water.

Makes about ½ cup

For glue you will need:

small pan

3 tablespoons water

stovetop or electric burner

1 package (¼ ounce) unflavored gelatin

mixing spoon

1 tablespoon white vinegar

1 teaspoon liquid glycerine (available at a drugstore)

glass jar with lid

How to do it:

1 In the pan, bring the water to a boil. Remove from heat and add gelatin, stirring to dissolve. Continue to stir and add the vinegar and glycerine. When the mixture has cooled, spoon it into the jar and cover.

2 When you are ready to use it, heat the glue by placing the glass jar in a pan of warm water (or heat in the microwave for 20–30 seconds).

3 To use, apply the glue with a brush. It takes a couple of days for the mixture to harden, so be patient.

Makes about ¼ cup

MIXING COLORS

Blue + yellow = green
Blue + red = purple
Red + yellow = orange
Red + white = pink
Blue + green = turquoise
Red + blue + green = brown

Use water-based paints (not oils), because they are much easier to clean up. Your choice of paint depends on what you're coloring. Poster paint is great for paper; fabric paint is needed for cloth. Acrylic paint is waterproof, so it, too, may be used on fabric. You can get great tints from watercolor paint, but it is more expensive than other kinds of paint and washes out easily. No matter what kind of paint you use, you don't need to buy every color of the rainbow. Remember that you can create colors by mixing paints.

Many of the projects, such as the greeting cards (see pages 111–113) and the African design (see pages 135–137), require **paper**. There are many kinds of papers, including some that are very expensive. In general, you don't need fancy papers. Make cards out of paper that is a little heavier than regular computer or copy paper, and create beautiful wrapping paper with paper that is a little bigger. **Newsprint**, for example, which doesn't cost very much and comes in very large sheets, and **butcher-block paper**, which is often sold by the roll, are perfect for wrapping-paper projects. For the hammering projects (see pages 106–109), the best paper to use is an absorbent one, such as the kind made for painting with watercolors. Cone-shaped **coffeemaker filters** are also good for hammering.

Tools

Even when you make things from nature, you'll need some basic tools. Fortunately, we don't have to make our own, though you probably could if you really needed to! Following is a list of basic tools needed to do the crafts in this book. There aren't many, but the right tool will make your crafting go much easier.

Cutting Tools

Often, before you can put things together, you have to cut things apart, or at least cut them to the right size and shape so they'll fit better.

Scissors come in all shapes, sizes, and prices, from blunt-ended children's scissors that cost less than a dollar (and that work surprisingly well) to fancy shears that can cost $100 or more. For cutting paper, ribbon, raffia, string, and cornhusks, a pair of child's craft scissors should do just fine. For cutting fabric and leather, you'll need a little better pair of scissors. To cut natural materials, such as sticks, pinecones, plant stems, and dried-flower stems, you will need garden snippers or shears.

A few of the projects require using a **knife**, but for most, a plastic knife will do. Polymer clay cuts easily with plastic, and a potato (for making the potato stamp; see page 174), depending on how ripe it is, may or may not cut with plastic. Even plastic knives can cut you, though, so be careful whenever you use a knife. Always cut away from yourself and your fingers. You may need to ask an adult or an older sibling to help. For a few of the wood projects, such as the totem pole (see page 38), you may need to use a **saw**, depending on how big your stick is. If you do, get an adult to do this part for you.

Tools for Heating and Mixing

Many of our projects require you to mix things, which makes **bowls** a necessary part of your toolbox. Buy inexpensive bowls to use just for crafts. Don't use the same bowls for cooking. Stainless-steel bowls are best, particularly for dyeing cloth, but plastic is fine for making paints and clay. Have a few sizes, ranging from small to large. **Pots** are necessary, too, for you'll be heating some of these mixtures on the stove.

If you do a lot of crafts that require a stove, your parents may be willing to purchase a small electric **burner** that you can use — with their supervision — in a basement or craft room. This keeps your craft projects separate from a cooking area, which is always helpful. Just be sure that you use a burner carefully and wisely, with adult supervision, and that there is plenty of air circulation in the room.

Other Tools

You'll need specific tools for certain projects. For example, a **funnel** is great for doing sand painting designs, and a **hammer** is a necessity for hammering flowers. **Clothespins** serve a surprising variety of purposes. For the most part, though, the projects in this book require very few tools.

Getting Organized

If you really love crafts, getting organized early in your career will set good work habits and will actually save you a lot of time. If you don't have to waste time looking for tools and materials, you'll have more time to spend making things.

Each artist has a different kind of **space** in which to work. Some may have a whole room; others will have only a desktop or part of a table. You're lucky if you have a spot that you can leave set up for your crafts, but if you don't, that's okay — you'll just have to be extra organized.

Make a **list** of the tools and materials you'll need for most of the projects. You'll probably need extra things for some projects, but put together a basic toolbox.

You'll also need a **box** for collecting natural treasures. This should be small enough for you to carry easily, and with a handle, if possible. Put a small **notebook** and **pencil** into the box so you can make notes about where and when you find things. After a collecting trip, divide your treasures into separate boxes, putting pinecones, for example, in one box and sticks and twigs in another.

TOOLBOX

Find a box big enough to hold all your basic tools. This is what you will need:

- **Several sheets of paper**
- **Markers, pencils**
- **Craft paints (at least red, yellow, blue)**
- **Paintbrushes**
- **Hot glue gun and glue sticks, craft glue, glue stick with liquid glue**
- **Adhesive tape (regular and removable)**
- **Craft scissors, fabric scissors**
- **Plastic knife**
- **Several strands of raffia**
- **Ruler**
- **Clipboard**
- **Clothespins, paper clips**
- **Paper towels**
- **Small hammer**

When you've finished using something, always put it back into the box.

Making Your Own Clay

There are many kinds of clay. Although I have included the information about the ancient art of making pottery clay, you might also enjoy this "newfangled" homemade clay recipe as well. You can let this air-dry, but it will harden better (and quicker) if you bake it in an oven at about 250°F. (This project requires adult supervision.)

You will need:

medium-size sauce pan

2 cups flour

2 cups water

1 cup salt

4 tablespoons vegetable oil

2 tablespoons cream of tartar

1 or 2 drops food coloring (optional)

mixing spoon

stovetop or electric burner

rolling pin

airtight container

How to do it:

1 In the pan, place the flour; water; salt; oil; cream of tartar; and food coloring, if desired. Mix thoroughly.

2 On the stove, warm the mixture over medium heat until it is a stiff batter but can easily be stirred. Remove from the heat and let cool.

3 When you can handle the dough comfortably, roll it into a ball. Flatten it with your hands and then roll it out with a rolling pin. With your hands, squish the dough together, then roll it out again. Finally, squish it over and over for a few minutes. If you want, add more food coloring as you knead it. Store in an airtight container.

Part Two

VINES,
twigs,
cones,
and moss

People who lived in or moved to the wilderness had to use what they could find to make what they needed. Think of it as going on a very long camping trip. There's a limited amount of stuff you can take with you. If you need something you haven't brought, or if you run out of something, you have to find it or make it. Luckily, nature is generous, and trees and plants grow all over the world except in some deserts, above the timberline on high mountains, and in the Arctic.

Tree Materials

Wherever they are found, trees have supplied materials to make things that people need, from houses to furniture, from toys to trinkets. Some trees, such as oaks, make excellent building material. Others, such as apple trees and palm trees, offer their fruit and seeds for us to eat.

Most of the projects in this section are best done with straight twigs and sticks. If you just can't get to a place where trees grow, all of these projects can be made with wooden skewers that you buy at the supermarket.

USING GLUE GUNS SAFELY

Most twig crafts require the use of a hot glue gun. You must be very careful when using a glue gun, and always get adult permission and supervision. See the important information about glue guns on page 7.

You can use regular glue for twig crafts, but projects will take a long time, because you must wait for the glue to dry before moving on to the next step.

Plant Materials

In addition, all kinds of plants have been used to make things. For example, vines of all sorts are woven into baskets. Anthropologists — scientists who study people — say that basket making is the oldest craft, meaning people have been weaving vines and reeds into baskets since ancient times. Baskets are used for carrying all kinds of things: nuts and berries, for example, meat from the hunt, and even water, if they are woven very tightly. Almost every region in the world has plants that are good for making baskets. Wherever you live, you can probably find plants that are good for weaving into baskets.

There are some places, such as the deserts, where plants don't grow very well. Yet people there still manage to find natural treasures from which they make utensils and shelter.

Although you won't have to build your house, make tools and utensils, and haul food and water, there are many crafts that use those same basic skills — they just don't take as long. Twigs and sticks, rather than logs, can be used to make picture frames, miniature furniture, and toys and games. Weave vines into beautiful pieces to hang in your window. Make lovable dolls and simple hats from cornhusks.

Vine Wreath *easy*

A huge number of plants can be woven to make items that are useful or pretty, or both. When you collect vines, choose ones that are thin enough to bend and tie easily, such as Virginia creeper, honeysuckle, kudzu, and wisteria — or anything else without thorns or briars.

You will need:

old sheet or towel

several lengths of bendable vine (for example, honeysuckle, wisteria, Virginia creeper, vinca)

1 jar or can at least 2½ inches in diameter (the size of the can determines the size of the wreath)

small twistie ties, if needed

craft glue, if needed

narrow ribbon, sheet moss, cones, and other decorative items

How to do it:

1 Cover your work area with a sheet or towel. Hold one end of a vine against the jar and wrap the vine around it twice, forming a double circle.

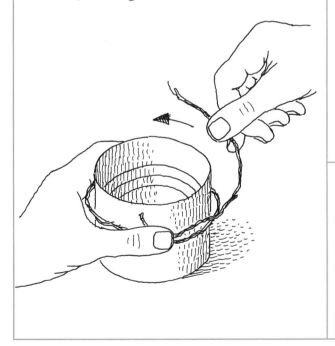

2 Slip the vine off the jar and begin to weave the long end of the rest of it over and under the circle to build the wreath. If you have trouble keeping the vine together, use twistie ties.

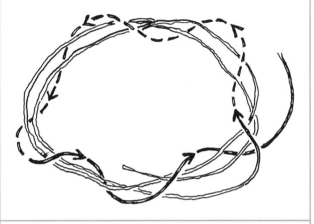

3 When you run out of vine, tuck the ends of the first piece into the weaving. Skip a small space, then tuck the end of a new piece into the weaving and continue with the over and under. Add vine until the thickness of the wreath pleases you. If you have trouble getting it to stay, use a dollop of glue.

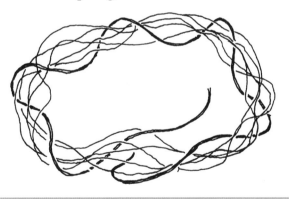

4 Decorate your wreath any way you like. You could glue on pinecones and moss for an autumn wreath or simply tie it with a ribbon. At Halloween, add some "spider webbing" and plastic spiders. In spring, tuck in some dried flowers for a colorful touch.

Vine-and-Twig Ball challenging

This can be a little tricky to get started, but keep at it. The results are wonderful. You can wrap a ball like this with mini holiday lights and hang it outside — it looks great. (This project requires adult supervision if you use spray varnish.)

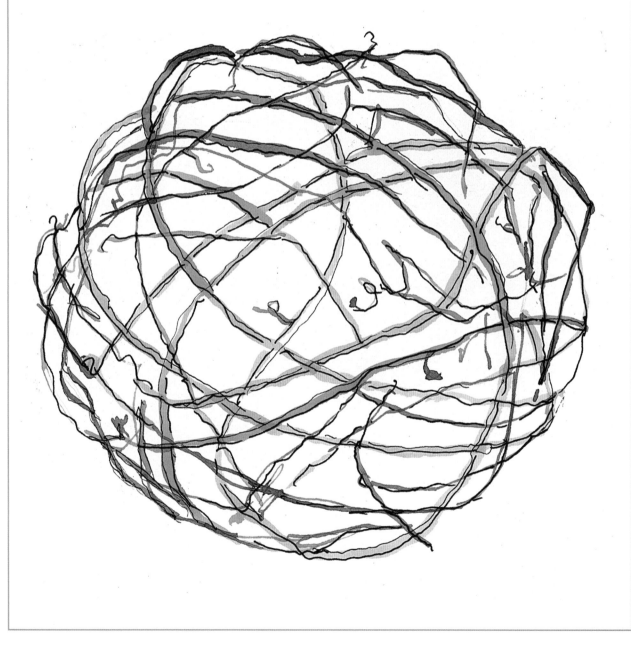

You will need:

old sheet or towel

medium-sized balloon

grocery bagful of vines

artist's wide paintbrush

craft glue

sharp pin or thumbtack

clear spray varnish (optional)

REMEMBER TO CONSERVE

Some trees are so useful — or so beautiful — that they have almost been used up. For example, mahogany has beautiful wood. European explorers found it growing in the West Indies island of Hispaniola. Not only was the wood beautiful, but it also was excellent for building everything from boats to pianos. People cut down so many of the trees that the native mahogany tree almost became extinct.

How to do it:

1 Cover your work area with a sheet or towel. Blow up the balloon, but leave it a little soft, so it won't pop as you work.

2 Take a long piece of vine and wrap it up and over the balloon one time, then tie it at the top. Don't cut the tails. Take another piece of vine and wrap it up and over the balloon in the other direction, making a cross at the top center. Tie. Leave the tails.

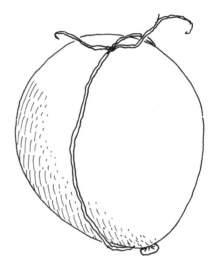

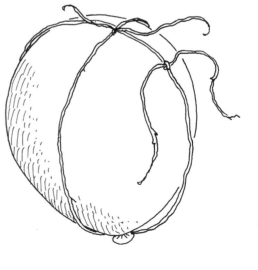

continued →

3 Take another piece of vine and tie one end to one of the vine pieces already on the balloon and pull it around the belly of the balloon. Weave the vine under other vine pieces whenever you get to them. When you get to the end of this piece, tie it off by attaching it to another piece. Continue to add vine pieces to cover the balloon, weaving in and out of any of the vines whenever you can. The more you weave your vines, the stronger the ball will be.

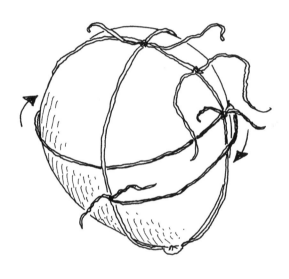

4 When you have added enough vines that you feel you're done, you'll still have lots and lots of empty spaces, but that's okay; it adds to the beauty of the ball.

5 Dip the paintbrush into the glue and paint over the vines. (Don't worry if the glue gets onto the balloon.) Try to get glue in the spots where several vines come together. The ball *should* stay together from your weaving — the glue is just added protection.

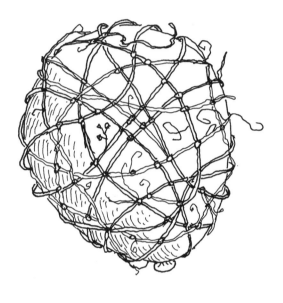

6 Allow the glue to dry, then pop the balloon with the pin. Fish out the balloon with the pin, if possible. Spray the ball with varnish, if desired.

Raffia Basket challenging

Raffia is extremely useful for tying things together in many crafts, but here it's used alone to make a beautiful little basket. All you do is braid six very long pieces of raffia (or 12 shorter pieces), then glue or sew the braid into a coiled basket. Sewing the coils together takes a long time, but the basket is soft and charming. Gluing is quicker and still looks nice.

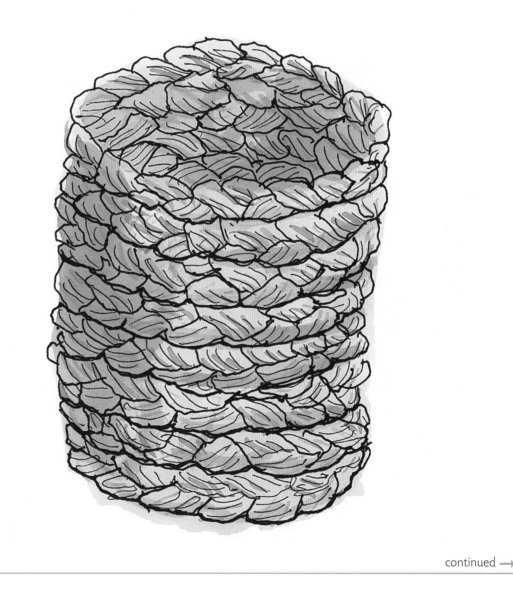

continued →

Raffia Basket

You will need:

old sheet or towel

at least 6 strands of very long or 12 strands of shorter raffia

clipboard

needle and thread, craft glue, or glue gun and glue stick (see Glue Gun Caution! on page 7)

small clothespins, if needed

scissors

TRAVEL LIGHT

Just for fun, pretend that you're going on a camping trip — and that you won't be coming back! Figure out how much you can carry in a backpack, then plan what to take with you. A lot depends on where you decide to go "camping." If you go to the ocean, you'll need certain things you wouldn't need if you were going to the mountains. Consider what each item weighs and then pack what will be most useful to you.

For example, if you decide to take seeds to plant, you'll have to figure out how long it will take for them to produce enough to eat. If you plan to hunt for food, what will you hunt and what will you hunt with? How will you collect and carry water? What will you sleep in — and under? There's a lot to think about!

How to do it:

1 Cover your work area with a sheet or towel. Tie six strands of raffia together at one end. Clip these to the top of a clipboard. Separate them into three groups of two strands each. (If using 12 strands of raffia, separate them into three groups of four strands each.)

2 Pull the strands on the left over the center strands. Hold them tightly in your left hand while you bring the right strands over the center strands. Holding those in your right hand, bring the left ones over the center, then the right ones, and so on. Be sure to pull down on the strands as you work to keep the braid straight.

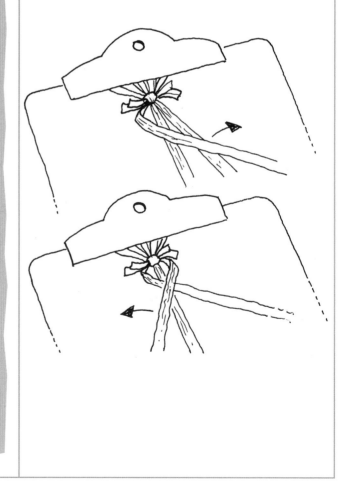

3 Braid the entire length of the raffia until you have a braid 40–48 inches long. When you reach the end, tightly tie the ends together.

4 Begin the coil by folding over one of the end knots and either sewing or gluing it to the braid next to it. Continue to coil the braid, sewing or gluing it together. If you are using glue, small clothespins will hold the braid until the glue dries.

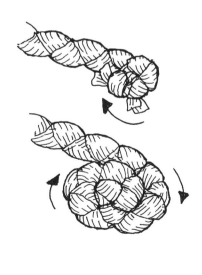

5 Keep coiling the braid until the bottom is at least 1½ inches across. Then begin to bring up the braid gradually, sewing or gluing the coil halfway up the coil below it until you can begin to attach the coil to the top of the piece just below it.

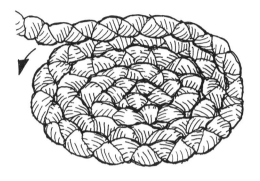

6 Keep the coils even so the basket won't look lopsided. Continue to coil until you have used all the braid. The basket should be 1¼–1½ inches tall. Leave a little bit of braid with the end knot and sew or glue tightly just below it to secure the coil, then snip off the end knot. Make sure the braid is attached securely so it won't come apart.

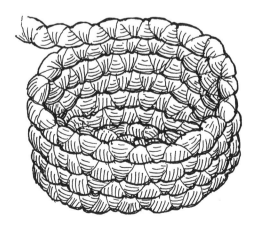

God's Eye challenging

This is a common kind of weaving that is found in many cultures. It is thought to have originated with the Huichol Indians in Jalisco, Mexico, but is found in Native American and African cultures, too. According to Mexican tradition, the four points of the cross are believed to represent earth, air, fire, and water. The first few steps are the hardest. Stick with it and as you get the hang of it, you'll find that the rest is very easy.

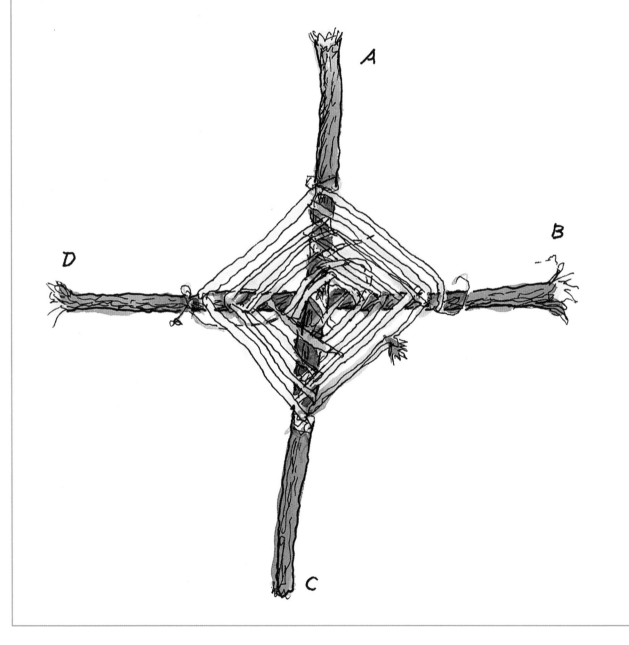

You will need:

old sheet or towel

2 sticks

long pieces of vine, raffia, yarn, string, or twine

craft glue or hot glue gun and glue stick, if needed (see Glue Gun Caution! on page 7)

How to do it:

1 Cover your work area with a sheet or towel. Place the sticks in a cross, with the upright piece on top.

2 Lay a vine across the upper-right corner, leaving about a 1-inch tail going toward the left. Weave it behind both sticks to the lower-left corner. Pull the vine across the front to the upper-right corner.

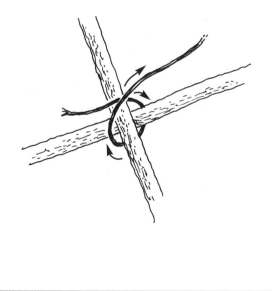

3 Pull the vine behind the right crosspiece and across the front to the upper left and behind the upper crosspiece.

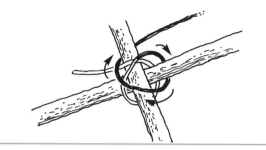

4 Go across the front to the lower left and behind the left crosspiece, then across the front to the lower-right corner.

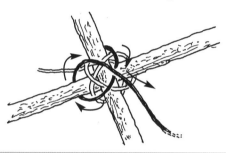

5 Go behind the lower upright piece, across the front to the upper-right corner, and behind the right crosspiece. Continue lashing, going to the far side of the next piece and looping around it, crossing in the center. As you continue and the X in the center widens, you'll begin to see a beautiful diamond pattern emerge.

6 When you come to the end of the vine, either add more vine (glue or tie it together so that it shows only in back) or simply tie or glue the end to the stick.

Picture Frame *easy*

Although constructing large things out of wood takes many large tools and a lot of time, you can create wonderful, smaller crafts just by using sticks thin enough to break with your hands. If you're fortunate enough to live near woods or a park, you'll probably find lots of twigs and small branches on the ground.

You will need:

old sheet or towel

ruler

plain picture frame with smooth, wide edges

plenty of twigs or sticks, all the same kind or different kinds

garden clippers, if needed

craft glue or hot glue gun and glue sticks (see Glue Gun Caution! on page 7)

sheet moss

small pinecones or dried flowers

How to do it:

1 Cover your work area with a sheet or towel. Measure the length of the picture frame. Then measure the glass across the top or bottom.

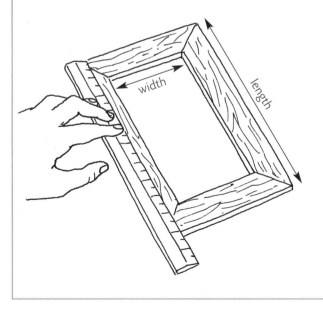

2 Break half the twigs so they are approximately the length of the frame. Break the rest of the twigs so they are the width of the glass. Use the clippers on any twigs that are too hard to break by hand.

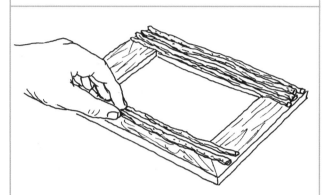

3 Arrange the twigs on the frame, covering it. Fit the short twigs between the long twigs. Beginning on one side, glue down each twig. Don't worry about gaps; place the twigs as close together as possible. When you have covered the sides, glue on the top and bottom pieces. It's fine if the twigs aren't all the same size or extend beyond the frame a little.

4 When the frame is covered, glue pieces of moss where there are gaps between the twigs. Decorate the frame with small pieces of pinecones or dried flowers. Insert your favorite picture. This makes a great gift!

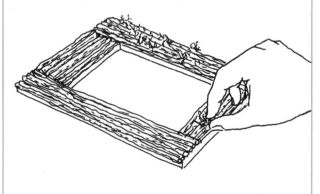

Chess Set medium

Making a game can be as much fun as playing it! These directions are for chess pieces, but you can also make checkers or tokens for tic-tac-toe. These same basic ideas apply to action figures, figures for a manger scene, or whatever you want.

The game of chess has two sets of 16 pieces each, for a total of 32 pieces. These instructions are for one twig set and one shell set. Each set contains one king, one queen, two bishops, two knights (these look like horses), two castles, and eight pawns. The game board consists of 64 squares.

king · queen · bishop · knight · castle · bishop · castle · knight · pawns · pawns · castle · knight · castle · pawns · king · bishop · knight · queen · bishop · knight · castle

For TWiG SET you will need:

old sheet or towel to cover work area

hot glue gun and glue sticks or craft glue (see Glue Gun Caution! on page 7)

twigs

moss

cornhusks

small stones

fungus

raffia

scissors

grass

ribbon, twine, or vine

8 tiny pinecones

NOTE

Many of these pieces need a base so they can stand by themselves. To create a base, make a 1-inch-square block from polymer clay. Press the twig or shell into the base to make just the right-sized hole, then remove. Bake the clay at 200°F for 8–10 minutes, or until hard. Then glue the twig or shell game piece into the hole and let dry.

How to make a castle:

Glue five 2-inch twigs together, making sure the bottom of the twigs are even, then top with a piece of moss.

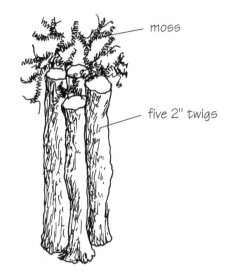

moss

five 2" twigs

How to make a knight:

Glue three twigs together to make the body. Glue a twig at one end for the neck, then add another twig for the head, and four twigs on the bottom for the legs. Add some moss for the tail and the mane.

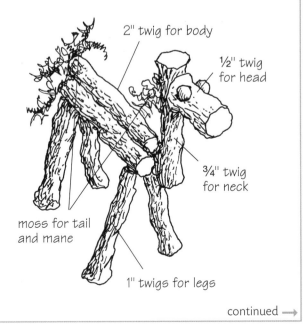

2" twig for body

½" twig for head

¾" twig for neck

moss for tail and mane

1" twigs for legs

continued →

Chess Set

How to make a king:

Glue a piece of cornhusk around a twig as a cape. Glue on a stone for the head, moss for hair, and a piece of fan-shaped fungus for a headdress.

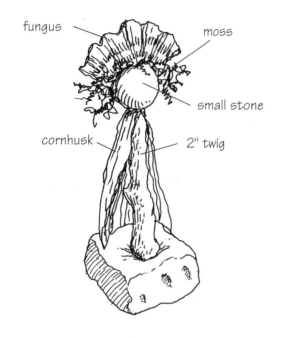

fungus

moss

small stone

cornhusk

2" twig

How to make a queen:

Glue a piece of cornhusk around a twig as a cape. Glue on a round stone for the head, grass for hair, and a piece of ribbon, twine, or vine for a crown.

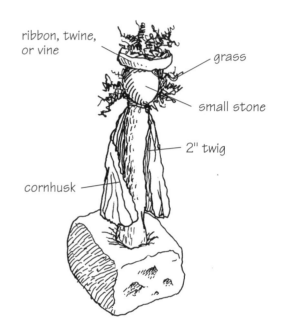

ribbon, twine, or vine

grass

small stone

2" twig

cornhusk

How to make a bishop:

Fold over the top of a cornhusk and tie it with a piece of raffia to make a "neck." Trim the bottom so it will stand up.

small piece of raffia

3" piece of cornhusk folded in half

How to make pawns:

Use eight small pinecones, each no longer than 1 inch.

For SHELL SET you will need:

old sheet or towel to cover work area

hot glue gun and glue sticks or craft glue (see Glue Gun Caution! on page 7)

shells: margarite, whelk, blue mussels, white dwarf clam-shells, limpet, spiky shells, scallop shells, and 9 small shells, such as coquinas (to identify shells, see page 211)

coral (available at craft stores)

sea creatures (available at craft stores)

How to make a castle:

Glue a flat-bottomed shell, such as a margarite, to the top of a piece of coral.

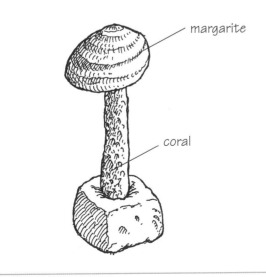

margarite

coral

How to make a knight:

If you can find them, use two tiny sea horses. If you can't find any, create horses from shells.

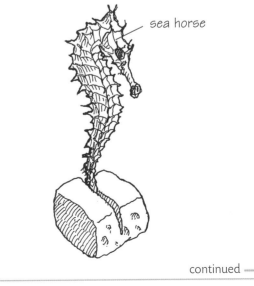

sea horse

continued →

Chess Set

How to make a king:

Glue two dwarf clamshells together to make a head and glue it to the top of a whelk. Add a shield, arm, and crown.

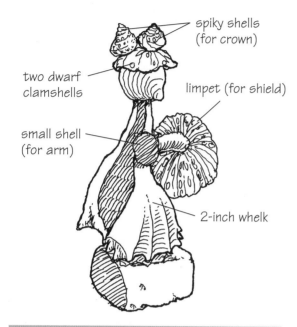

spiky shells (for crown)

two dwarf clamshells

limpet (for shield)

small shell (for arm)

2-inch whelk

How to make a bishop:

Glue two blue mussels to each other, then glue a dwarf clamshell to the top, narrow end.

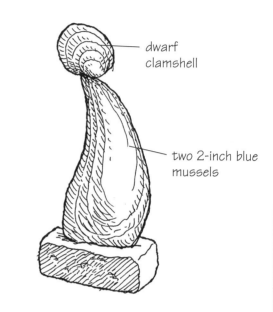

dwarf clamshell

two 2-inch blue mussels

How to make a queen:

Glue two dwarf clamshells together to make a head and glue it to the top of a whelk. Add a robe and crown.

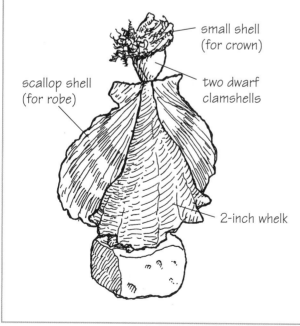

small shell (for crown)

scallop shell (for robe)

two dwarf clamshells

2-inch whelk

How to make pawns:

Select eight small shells for the pawns.

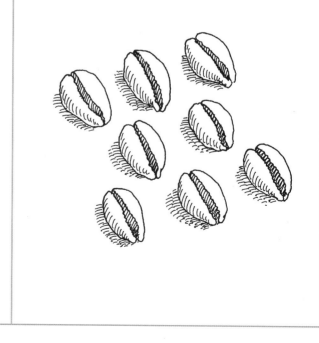

Mini Woodland Furniture _medium_

You can make great little pieces of furniture out of twigs for a fairy or gnome home or for a dollhouse. Ornamented with dried flowers, nuts, or leaves, they make wonderful little decorations for your room. These are just some ideas; use what you can find and your imagination!

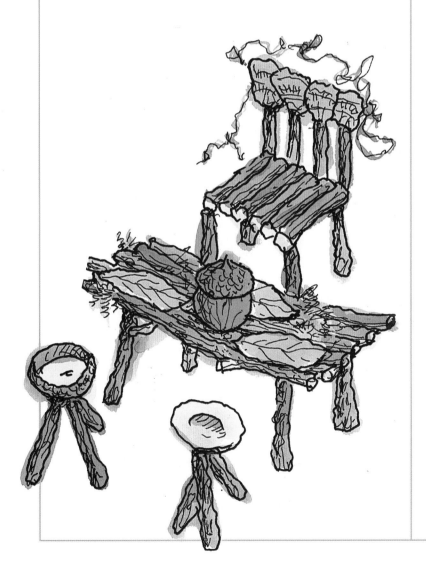

You will need:

old sheet or towel to cover work area

27–29 small twigs or sticks

garden clippers

hot glue gun and glue sticks or craft glue (see Glue Gun Caution! on page 7)

sheet moss

bark

acorn, peach pit, or flat stone

How to make a table:
Cut or break six twigs to the same length (about 4 inches is good) and glue them together to make the tabletop. Fill in cracks with moss. Cut or break four small twigs for the legs and glue one to each corner.

How to make a chair:
Cut or break six twigs to the same length and glue them together to make the seat. Glue four twigs at right angles to the seat to make the chair back. Glue bark and curly twigs across the top for decoration. Cut or break four small twigs for the legs and glue one to each corner.

How to make a stool:
Cut or break three twigs to the same length and glue them together to form a tripod. Glue an upside-down acorn, half a peach pit, or a stone for the seat.

Stick Animals

medium

You'll have great fun creating animals out of sticks and moss. The best part is coming up with your own ideas, but here are some to get you started. Look at a picture book of animals and try to figure out what makes one animal different from another. For example, antlers make a horse figure look like a reindeer. Curled antlers make the same figure look like a mountain sheep. A curved tail makes another figure look like a wolf. Use moss, cones, seeds — anything you want — to make the figures more recognizable, but try to use all natural materials.

You will need:

old sheet or towel to cover work area

selection of twigs

hot glue gun and glue sticks or craft glue (see Glue Gun Caution! on page 7)

pinecones

sheet moss or lichen

raffia

scissors

NOTE

It is better to use twigs that you find on the ground than to cut green ones. Not only do they break more easily, but also they are already dried and will not shrink. Of course, you don't want to cut a living tree. If the bark is not firmly attached, scrape it off the twigs before you begin your project. Otherwise, the bark will slip off the twig and your project could fall apart.

How to make a horse:

Follow the instructions for making a twig knight (see page 29), but use three thin twigs about 3 inches long and glue them together to create the body. The neck should be about 1 inch long, the legs 1–1½ inches long, and the head ½–¾ inch long.

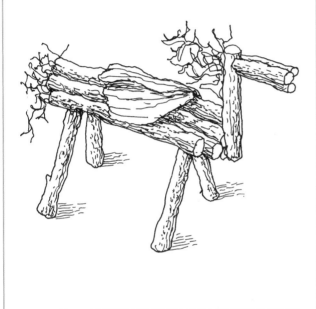

How to make a reindeer:

Make a body just as you did for the horse but with a smaller head. Do not add a mane. Affix a tiny piece of twig, standing upright, for the tail. Add "antlers" by gluing tiny, branched twigs to the head.

How to make a porcupine:

Use a bristly pinecone and add tiny legs and ears made out of pieces of moss or lichen.

How to make a snail:

To make the body, coil a piece of braided raffia (see pages 22–23) and glue it to secure the spiral. Cut off the ends to make the antlers.

Twig Basket medium

The size of your basket depends on the size of your sticks or twigs. Smaller baskets can be built out of smaller twigs. Be sure to scrape off any loose bark before you begin.

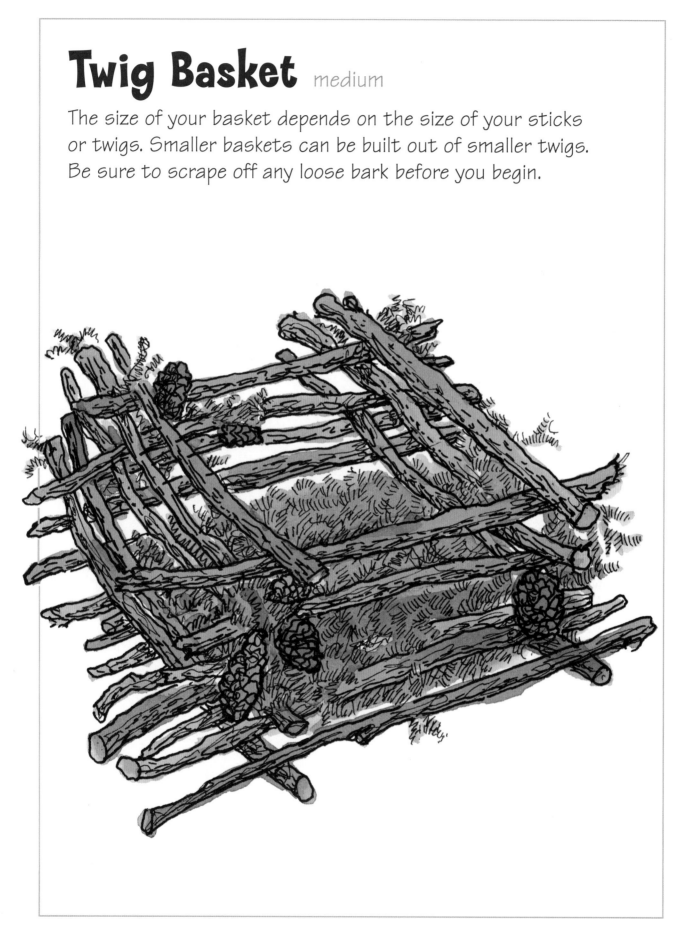

You will need:

old sheet or towel

20–24 straight sticks or twigs

hot glue gun and glue sticks or craft glue (see Glue Gun Caution! on page 7)

sheet moss (optional)

pinecones (optional)

vines (optional)

How to do it:

1 Cover your work area with a sheet or towel. Place two sticks 4–8 inches apart. This is a good distance if your twigs are about ½ inch in diameter. If they are smaller, place them closer together.

Place two more sticks on top of these, making a square. Allow the sticks to extend about 1 inch on all sides. Glue the top sticks to the bottom sticks.

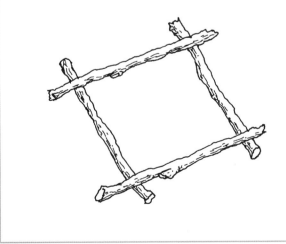

2 Take several more sticks and glue them next to the top sticks, leaving a little space between each one. This makes the base for your basket.

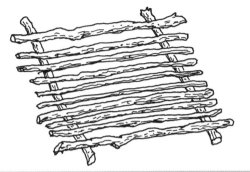

3 Glue on two more sticks, on top of the base at each side, in line with the first two bottom sticks. Continue to add sticks two at a time, building a little "log cabin." Keep adding sticks until the basket is as tall as you'd like, maybe 4–5 inches tall.

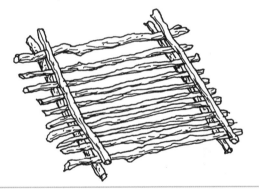

4 Decorate the basket with moss and cones, if you'd like, or put a layer of moss on the bottom. For an even more rustic touch, add a vine handle, gluing or weaving it into the twigs.

Totem Pole medium

Totem poles were originally carved from cedar trees by Native Americans living in the Pacific Northwest. There are basically four kinds of totem poles:

- **crest poles** tell about a family's ancestors
- **history poles** tell the history of a clan or village
- **legend poles** illustrate famous myths or stories
- **memorial poles** tell about an important person within a village or clan.

Totem poles carved by people from Haida and Tlingit villages in the Pacific Northwest were huge — up to 50 feet. They were almost always carved out of cedar because the wood was so hard that it could withstand the rainy and snowy weather.

Despite the old phrase "low man on the totem pole," which means somebody new or inexperienced, the lowest figure on a totem pole was actually the most important, because that was the one seen most clearly. The most experienced artist always carved the bottom figure.

You will need:

old sheet or towel

polymer clay

smooth stick

sandpaper

pencil

paper, if needed

paintbrushes

acrylic paints

COMMON DESIGNS

Some common animals carved on totem poles include:

THUNDERBIRD: Found at the top of many totem poles; stands for power

RAVEN: Stands for mystery

EAGLE: Means clear vision

BEAR: Symbolizes strength

WOLF: Stands for commitment

bear   wolf

How to do it:

1 Cover your work area with a sheet or towel. Make a clay base for your totem pole so that it will be able to stand by itself (see the Note box on page 29).

2 Peel the bark off the stick. Use sandpaper to smooth the edges.

3 Draw your design on the stick with the pencil (you may want to practice on paper first). I've included some easy traditional designs you can copy, or make up your own. Or create a totem pole with every member of your family represented.

4 Fill in the design using acrylic paints, which work well on wood. Let the paint dry thoroughly.

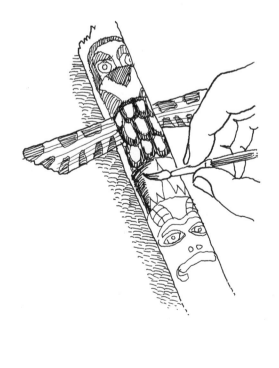

Woodland Basket medium

A fun way to make a stunning woodland basket is to use an inexpensive, store-bought basket as a base. Baskets with flat sides are a little easier to work with than those with curved sides. Glue all kinds of treasures onto it and you'll have a beautiful piece of art.

You will need:

old sheet or towel

hot glue gun and glue sticks or craft glue (see Glue Gun Caution! on page 7)

woodland treasures: cones, nuts, pieces of dried flowers, seeds and pits, balls from the sweet-gum tree, bark

inexpensive basket

green sheet moss or Spanish moss (optional)

WOODLAND TREASURES

The woods are a wonderful place to pick up interesting tidbits to use for decorations. Pinecones — and cones from other evergreen trees — often come in handy. Nuts and seedpods are great, too. A walk through the woods always turns up things you can use. Be respectful, though, and don't pull up or take anything that would leave a scar in the woods. Use only what is abundant and readily available.

How to do it:

1 Cover your work area with a sheet or towel. Think about your design before you begin gluing.

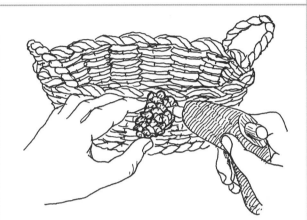

2 Using the hot glue gun, attach various woodland treasures to the basket to create a nice design. It's good to use large treasures to help cover the basket quickly, then glue smaller ones on top of those. Work one section at a time, overlapping the natural material so that it covers the basket.

3 If desired, line the inside of the basket with green sheet moss or a thin layer of Spanish moss.

Woodland Creatures medium

You can make any number of woodland creatures with cones and pods. Wrap a piece of fishing wire around them and hang them in the window, let them adorn the Christmas tree, or just line them up across a shelf in your room. They'll bring you the luck of the forest. Use whatever is available to you; following are just some suggestions.

You will need:

old sheet or towel to cover work area

scissors

poppy seedpod

hot glue gun and glue sticks or craft glue (see Glue Gun Caution! on page 7)

Spanish moss

small twigs

bark

cornhusk

small pinecones

large pinecone bracts (scales)

small brown nuts or cones

acorn tops

raffia

cotton boll

How to make an elf:

Cut the seedpod's stem 1½ inches from the head. Glue on Spanish moss for hair. Glue on twigs for arms and legs and bark for a shirt and pants. Add a cornhusk hat and pinecone shoes.

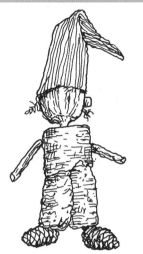

How to make a fairy:

Glue a small pinecone to the top of a larger one to make the head and body. Add strands of Spanish moss for hair and two pinecone bracts for fairy wings.

How to make a gnome:

Cut two pieces of bark into a fan shape and glue them to the front and back of a twig to make a "shirt." Add a nut for the head, small twigs for arms and legs, bits of bark for shoes, an acorn cap, and a raffia tie.

How to make an angel:

Glue a nut to the top of a thick twig to make a head and body. Cut a cotton boll in half and glue to the back for wings. Add moss for hair.

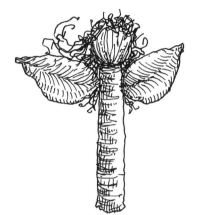

WHO'S WHO?

The fanciful world of small woodland creatures can be a little confusing. Here are a few definitions that may help sort things out:

DWARF: Short, stocky man who lives in dark woods and often works with metal.

ELF: A tiny woodland creature who gets into mischief.

FAIRY: Small or large beautiful creature with wings. Fairies can be either good or bad to humans.

GNOME: Short, stocky man or woman with long hair and a large hat. You'll usually find gnomes near large rocks or in lawns and gardens.

PIXIE: A kind of fairy, usually with red hair, who lives in fields.

Bark and Moss House *challenging*

Fanciful creatures from the woods and forests need a place to live. Help them out by building tiny houses out of woodland materials. Think of what would make them comfortable.

This house has a slanted roof and is made from all natural materials, particularly bark. Never take bark or moss off a living tree. You'll need to find bark from a fallen log or a large stick and buy sheet moss or Spanish moss from a craft store. Sometimes you can get large pieces of bark from people who sell firewood. If you can't find the right kind of bark, come up with some other kind of building material.

old sheet or towel

2 or 3 large pieces of bark at least 2½ inches wide

garden clippers or heavy scissors

hot glue gun and glue sticks or craft glue (see Glue Gun Caution! on page 7)

ruler

twigs

sheet moss or Spanish moss

How to do it:

1 Cover your work area with a sheet or towel. The shape of your house will depend on the shape of the bark you find. If it's flat, your house will be square. If it's rounded, your house will be round.

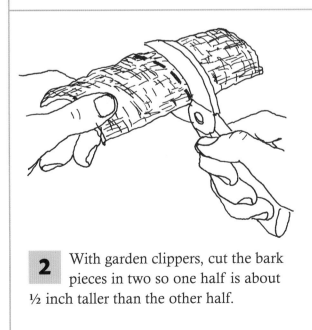

2 With garden clippers, cut the bark pieces in two so one half is about ½ inch taller than the other half.

3 Glue the bark pieces together to form the walls of the house. Because the roof is at a slanted angle, the walls on one side of the house need to be shorter than the walls on the other side. Overlap the bark, if necessary. Add extra pieces of bark as needed.

4 Use the clippers to cut a door out of one of the walls.

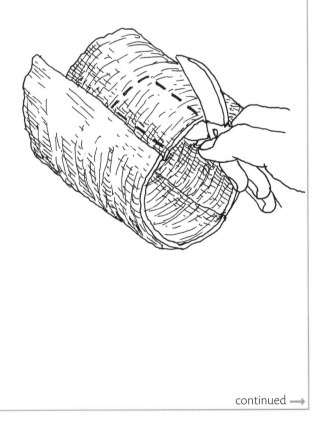

continued ➞

Bark and Moss House

5 With a ruler, measure across the top of the house and cut or break twigs to that size. The twigs in the middle of the roof need to be longer than the twigs on the ends.

6 Lay the twigs one at a time across the top of the house, slanting the roof from the tall walls to the shorter ones. Glue the twigs to one another and to the tops of the bark walls. Use moss to fill any holes in the roof.

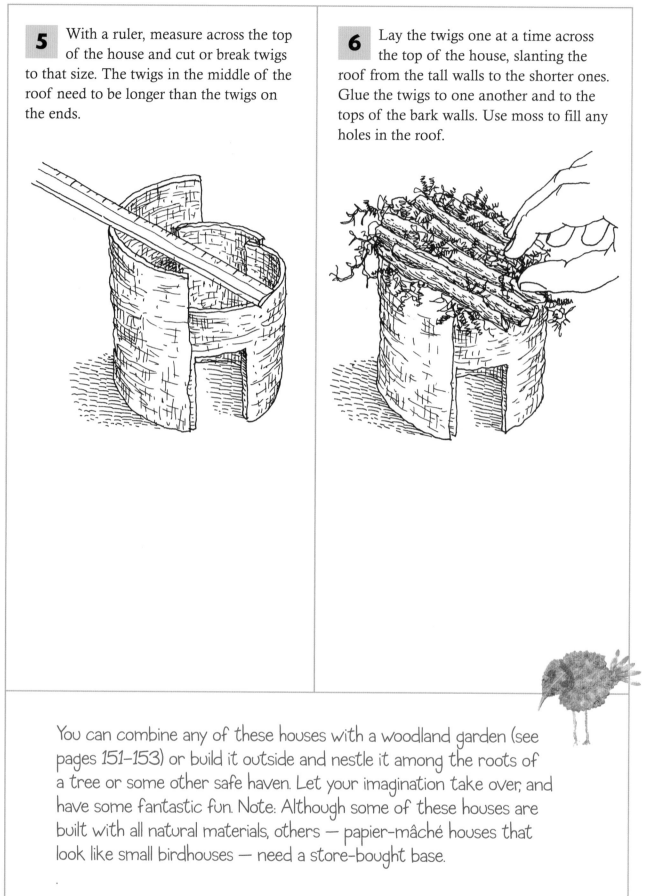

You can combine any of these houses with a woodland garden (see pages 151–153) or build it outside and nestle it among the roots of a tree or some other safe haven. Let your imagination take over, and have some fantastic fun. Note: Although some of these houses are built with all natural materials, others — papier-mâché houses that look like small birdhouses — need a store-bought base.

Spanish Moss House medium

If you live in the South, you may be able to collect Spanish moss yourself — just make sure you brush all the bugs out of it before you begin your project! If you live anywhere else, you can easily buy Spanish moss at a craft store. This moss is gray and curly and kind of woody rather than soft and green. It makes a wonderful little house.

continued →

Spanish Moss House

old sheet or towel

large handful of Spanish moss

sturdy flat piece of bark, about 2 inches by 4½ inches

hot glue gun and glue sticks or thick craft glue (see Glue Gun Caution! on page 7)

wooden skewer or pencil

at least 8 twigs

garden clippers or heavy scissors

small, thin piece of bark

acorn top or other nut

lichen

How to do it:

1 Cover your work area with a sheet or towel. Take a ball of Spanish moss in your hands and begin to make a nest out of it, pushing in the center to form a bowl. Keep working the moss into a bowl shape.

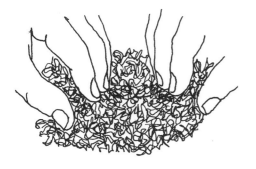

2 Place the moss bowl facedown on the large piece of bark. Glue down three quarters of the moss bowl, leaving an unglued space for the door.

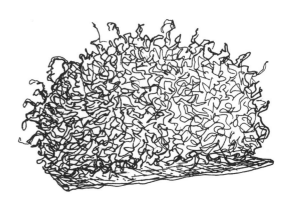

3 Use the wooden skewer to push out a door.

4 When you have a good door opening, cut (or break) two twigs so they are approximately the same height as the opening. Cut (or break) one shorter twig to fit across the top of the door opening.

7 At the back of the house, use the wooden skewer to push out some moss to make a small window.

5 Glue the two longer twigs upright on each side of the door opening, making the sides of the door frame. Glue the shorter piece to the tops of the upright twigs to complete the frame.

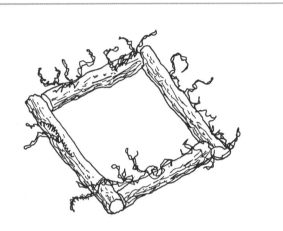

8 Make a window frame by cutting (or breaking) four small twigs and gluing them together to form a square. Glue on some lichen for decoration.

6 Cut a piece of thin bark to the size of the door frame; this is the door. Glue on the acorn top for a doorknob. Glue one side of the door to the frame. You can glue it all the way shut, all the way open, or partway open.

9 Glue the window frame to the edges of the opening in the moss. If it doesn't seem secure, use another twig for support, gluing one end to the bottom of the window and the other end to the bark base.

If desired, glue together twigs to make a chimney, front steps, a path leading to the front door, or a twig bench just outside the door (see the table on page 33 — it could double as a bench).

Pinecone-Roof Cottage challenging

This is a neat little cottage that begins with a cardboard base. You can make this any size you want, of course, but it takes a long time to do the roof, so it's a good idea to start small. *Note:* A hot glue gun and glue sticks are necessary; regular glue won't work for this project.

You will need:

old sheet or towel

garden clippers

1 or 2 pinecones with large bracts (scales)

cardboard birdhouse base (available at most craft stores), approximately 3 inches tall. The roof should peak in the middle like an upside-down V.

hot glue gun and glue sticks (see Glue Gun Caution! on page 7)

bark

scissors

green sheet moss

wooden skewer

How to do it:

1 Cover your work area with a sheet or towel. With the clippers, cut or pull off lots of bracts (scales) from the pinecones.

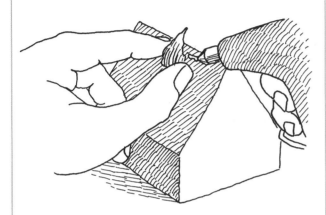

2 Start at one edge of the roof's peak. Place glue on the roof about the width of one of the bracts. Glue the bract to the roof, making the pointed end of the bract even with the top of the roof. Glue another bract right next to this, and so on, making a line across the top of the roof.

3 Start the next line of bracts, placing the first bract between the first two bracts on the line above.

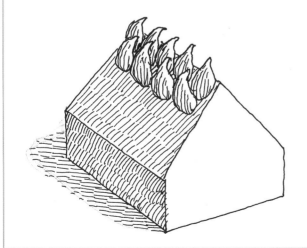

4 Continue placing rows of bracts so that the tip of each one goes between the upper two. When the side of the roof is covered, repeat steps 2 through 4 on the other side.

5 Flatten out the pieces of bark, if necessary, and cut them to fit the sides of the house. If there is not a door in the cardboard house, cut one out. (Make sure the bark doesn't cover the door opening.) Glue the bark to the sides of the house.

6 Fill in the gaps in the roof by pushing green moss down into the holes with a wooden skewer. Apply glue, as needed. Cover any gaps or holes in the bark walls by gluing on pieces of moss.

Moss and Cornhusk House medium

Build this same type of house, only a little larger, and hang it up for a birdhouse. If you do this, make sure your materials are waterproof and will survive wind and rain. Use pieces of wood for the base and paint the cornhusk roof with a waterproof coating.

You will need:

old sheet or towel

hot glue gun and glue sticks or craft glue (see Glue Gun Caution! on page 7)

2 wide cornhusks

round cardboard house base, about 3 inches tall and 2½ inches across, with a round roof

raffia

scissors

green sheet moss

How to do it:

1 Cover your work area with a sheet or towel. Glue the cornhusks, placing their narrow ends together, so that when they are spread out they cover the roof of the cardboard house.

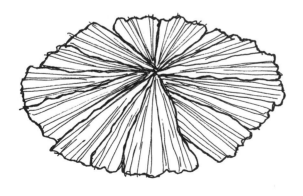

2 Gather together the ends at the top and tie a piece of raffia around them to form a little bundle.

3 Fan out the husks and place the bundle over the roof. Cut the husks so the edges overhang the roof a little bit.

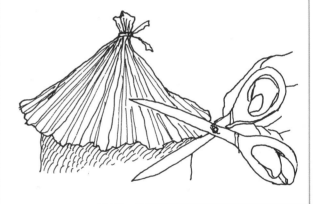

4 Remove the husks, apply glue to the cardboard roof, and stick the husks down. Cut a door in the side of the house if it doesn't already have one. Glue the moss to the sides of the house.

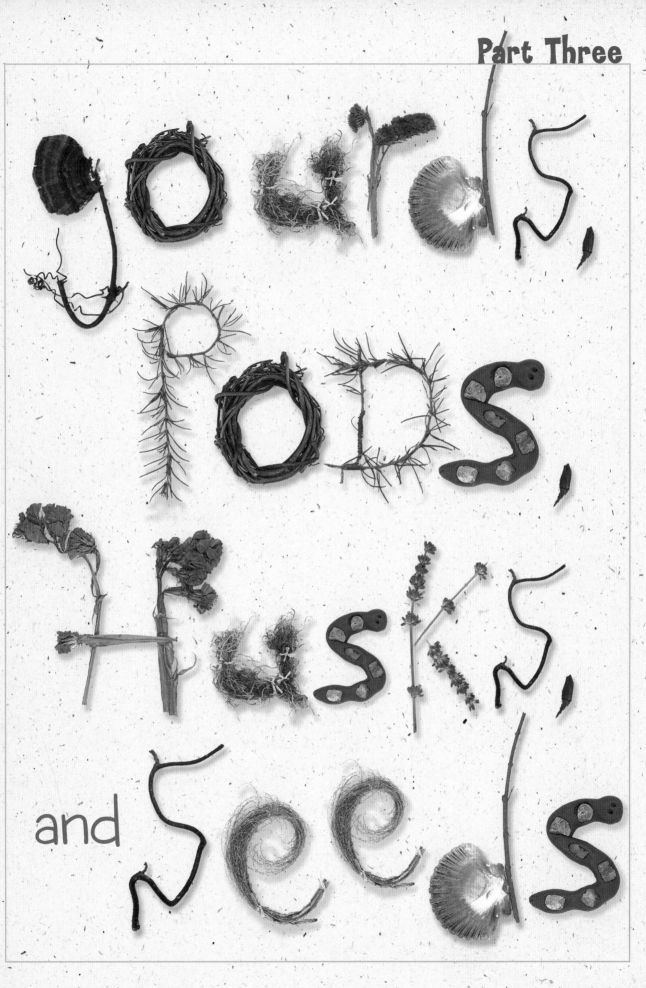

gourds, Pods, Husks, and Seeds

Although we usually think about the most useful parts of plants as being either food or flowers, other parts can also be quite useful. Some ancient civilizations, such as that of the Inca (in Peru) and those of some Native American tribes, grew squashlike vegetables called gourds. Even though gourds were not good to eat, they could use the hard shell as a container. You can turn a gourd into a Native American buffalo rattle, similar to one used in traditional ceremonies (see page 60). Okra, a vegetable of the American South, when left on the vine produces beautiful ribbed pods, which can be turned into lovely decorations.

Corn for Art

Corn was so important to many Native American tribes that they considered the plant itself to be sacred. Myths and stories abound in which corn is called a god. A number of tribes depended almost entirely on corn for food; if the corn crop failed, they starved. Because of this, they took great care to plant the corn seed with much ceremony and prayer.

The greatest celebrations took place in fall, when the corn ripened and was harvested. The Iroquois celebrated the Great Corn Festival, 1 the Southeast, the Green

Corn Dance was the most sacred holiday of the year.

People sometimes wore masks during these ceremonies. Although some masks were carved from wood, others were made out of woven or braided cornhusks. Probably the most common toy among the Native American people of the American Southwest was a cornhusk doll. As you work with your cornhusk projects, don't forget that you can dye the husks, too. For instructions, see pages 122–126.

see pages 122–126.

A"MAIZE"ING CORN

Early pioneers used corn for a number of purposes, including making corn whiskey (reputedly just to treat coughs, colds, toothaches, rheumatism, and arthritis), corn syrup, corn oil, and corn starch. Between 1790 and 1840, it was estimated that each American adult consumed 5 gallons of corn whiskey each year. Corn cobs were used for making pipes, tool handles, hair curlers, and checkers.

Today, corn is used to make an astonishing number of products, including:

Aspirin	Jelly
Bandages	Ketchup
Cardboard	Marshmallows
Charcoal briquettes	Paper
Chewing gum	Pie filling
Cosmetics	Shoe polish
Crayons	Soap
Diapers	Soda
Fireworks	Wallpaper
Glue	

Seeds for Art

There are countless kinds, sizes, and shapes of seeds, including fruit pits and beans. Some seeds, such as poppy seeds, are so tiny that they look like specks of dust. Other seeds are huge (think of a coconut). You can find seeds everywhere — inside fruits and vegetables, in dried soup mixes, outside in nature — just look around! Many seeds are beautiful and colorful and are great for using in crafts.

Gourd Doll *easy*

Gourds may be the strangest-looking vegetable that ever grew. Many are funny shapes and some are covered with bumps and warts. Wherever the gourd was found growing, native peoples found plenty of uses for them. Some gourds are hollow and waterproof and have a wonderful smooth outer layer, making them perfect for bowls and pots. Others were used as rattles and decorations. They also make great dolls, as long as you don't mind very *loooong* noses!

You will need:

old sheet or towel

scissors

piece of white fabric at least 6 inches long

craft glue, hot glue gun and glue sticks, or needle and thread (see Glue Gun Caution! on page 7)

handful of cotton balls or stuffing

string or raffia

paintbrush

acrylic paints

small gourd with a long, curved stem

pieces of sheet moss, yarn, embroidery thread, or corn silk

How to do it:

1 Cover your work area with a sheet or towel. With the scissors, cut the fabric so that it is 6 inches long and 2½ inches wide.

2 Fold the fabric in half lengthwise. Glue along the bottom and side edges, forming a bag. Allow it to dry. (You can sew instead of glue, if you prefer.)

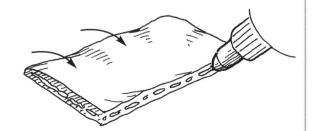

3 Turn the fabric bag inside out. Place a small amount of stuffing in the bag. Tie the string loosely around the top of the bag, gathering in the top.

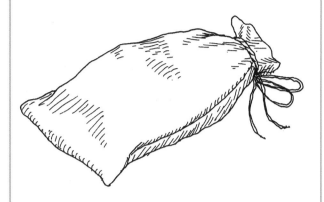

4 Paint a face on the gourd, using the long, curved stem as a nose. Glue small bits of moss or other material to the top of the head for hair.

5 Glue the gourd to the bag, with the "nose" pointing outward.

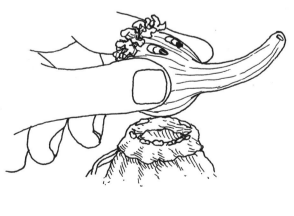

Gourd Buffalo Rattle *easy*

Buffalo supplied almost everything needed by the tribes of the American Southwest. Red Cloud, a Sioux leader, called the buffalo a sacred gift to his people. Because of the tribes' need and respect for the buffalo, they devised many prayers, rituals, and ceremonies that involved the animal. Rattles painted to look like buffalo were used in those ceremonies.

BUFFALO USES

All parts of the buffalo (more correctly called *bison*) were used for something.

BONES: Arrowheads, knives, other tools

HAIR: Rope, halters

HIDE (tanned): Moccasins, bedding, clothing, tepee lining

HIDE (raw): Glue

HORNS: Bowls, spoons

MUSCLES: Thread, bowstring

TAIL: Flyswatter

TONGUE: Meat, hairbrush

You will need:

old sheet or towel

rounded gourd with a long handle, seeds still inside

soap and water

pencil

acrylic paints

paintbrush

2 okra pods, curved at the ends (about the same size), or 2 curved sticks

hot glue gun and glue sticks or craft glue (see Glue Gun Caution! on page 7)

raffia, twine, or thin vines

How to do it:

1 Cover your work area with a sheet or towel. Clean the gourd with soap and water. Allow it to dry thoroughly in the sun.

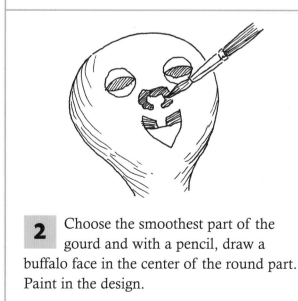

2 Choose the smoothest part of the gourd and with a pencil, draw a buffalo face in the center of the round part. Paint in the design.

3 Glue the okra pods to the sides of the gourd. These are the horns.

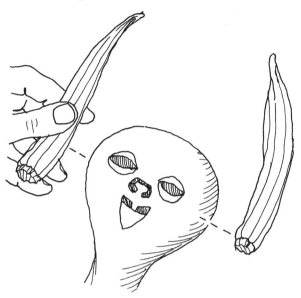

4 Choose four or five strands of raffia. Fold down about 2 inches and place the fold at the back of the rattle, at the top of the "stem" and just under the "head." Begin to wrap the long strands of raffia around the stem, securing the loose ends as you wrap over them. Wrap the raffia around the stem tightly, going down the stem and keeping the raffia in a single layer. When you reach the end of the raffia, tie together the loose ends and glue them securely to the back of the stem.

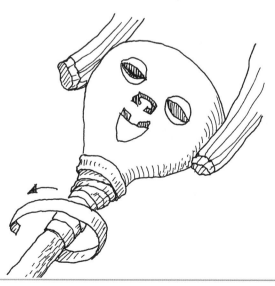

Okra Pod Canoe and People *easy*

Okra, a vegetable of the American South, when left on the vine, produces beautiful ribbed pods. An okra pod is the same shape as a canoe, making this an easy — but real-looking — project. Add a couple of stick figures to row the boat, and it's a great piece if you love boats and water. If you prefer to make a raft instead of a canoe, just glue twigs together (as you did for the tabletop on page 33), give the stick figures legs, and glue them to the raft.

You will need:

old sheet or towel

long, curved okra pod or other similarly shaped seedpod, such as a milkweed pod

hot glue gun and glue sticks or craft glue (see Glue Gun Caution! on page 7)

assortment of twigs

small nuts, seeds, or pieces of bark

How to do it:

1 Cover your work area with a sheet or towel. Hold the okra pod so that the curve at the end points upward. With your finger, carefully take out the center "rib" of the pod to hollow it out a little. No matter what kind of pod you're using, you'll need to carve out space for the inside of the canoe. *Note:* If the pod begins to split, "caulk" it, or fill the cracks with glue.

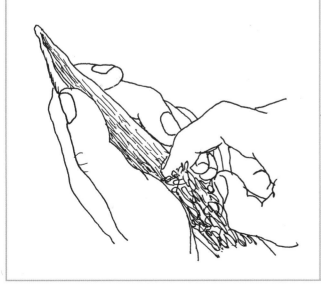

2 Break two twigs so they are short enough to look like people sitting in the canoe. To make their heads, glue nuts, seeds, or bark to the tops of the twigs. Break four twigs for arms, and glue two arms to each body.

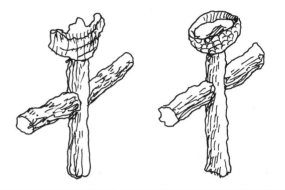

3 Break two smaller twigs for the paddle handles. Glue small pieces of bark to one end of each paddle. With the paddles in the "water," glue the handle of the paddle to the right arm of one figure and the handle of the other paddle to the left arm of the other figure.

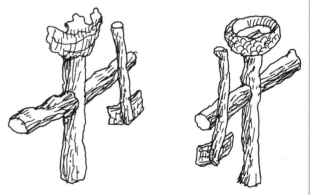

4 Place the figures in the boat, one at the bow, one at the stern. Glue them in place.

Cornhusk Hat *easy*

Although it takes lots of cornhusks, this "chapeau" is quite simple to make. The husks tend to shrink a little as they dry, so be sure to make this hat big enough to fit on your head. You can decorate the brim with anything you like. Try a couple of feathers or a band of dried flowers. As you work with your cornhusks, don't forget that you can dye the husks. For instructions, see pages 122–126.

You will need:

old sheet or towel

20–30 field cornhusks, depending on how wide they are (they must be at least 10 inches long)

large pan of water

4–6 paper towels

craft glue or hot glue gun and several glue sticks (see Glue Gun Caution! on page 7)

7 long pieces of raffia or 1 piece of raffia and 1 long piece of rope or ribbon

small to medium-sized bowl (about the same size as your head)

smaller bowl that fits on top of the medium bowl

scissors

large feather or other ornaments, for decorations

CORNHUSKS

The husks from field corn are thicker and bigger than husks from garden corn and, therefore, better for crafts. Or just use the ones you pull off an ear of corn that you're going to eat. These are usually small and green, but they'll work for most projects. You can buy cornhusks in the produce department of most supermarkets; they are used for making Mexican tamales. Cornhusks are much easier to work with if you first soak them in water. This makes them flexible and less likely to tear.

How to do it:

1 Cover a flat work area with a sheet or towel. Separate the cornhusks and place them in the pan of water. Soak them for 3 to 4 minutes. Take the husks out of the water and place them on paper towels. Let them dry for a few minutes so they are still damp but not really wet.

2 Place a damp (but not wet) husk on your work area. On a second husk, put a long, thin stream of glue along the long side. Overlap the two husks and glue them together, placing the narrow tips at the same end.

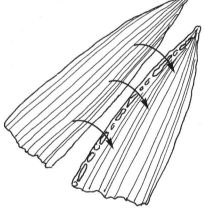

3 Continue to overlap and glue husks, allowing the narrow ends to come to a point in the center. Don't worry if the wide ends are not the same length; you'll fix that later.

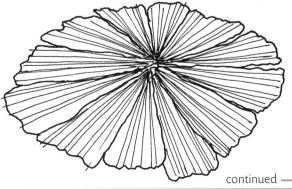

continued →

Cornhusk Hat

4 When you have completed the circle and overlapped the last husk over the first, stand the hat upright. Tightly tie a piece of raffia about 1 inch from the top of the hat, creating a topknot.

5 Turn the larger bowl upside down. Place the hat over the bowl, with the topknot pointing up. Gently push the hat over the bowl to curve it. Be careful not to tear the husks. Take the smaller bowl and place it on top of the other, with the hat in between to help keep it on the bowl as it dries.

6 Braid six strands of raffia into a hatband (see pages 22–23 for instructions on braiding raffia). Or you can use a piece of rope or ribbon instead. Place the hatband around your head, as if it had a hat in it. Add 3 to 4 inches to the band, then cut it with scissors. Tie the two ends together and try on the band again. If it doesn't fit perfectly, make it larger or smaller as needed.

7 Remove the small bowl from on top of the hat and place the hatband over the hat on the larger bowl as illustrated. Push it down until it fits just right over the hat, then glue it in place. Push on the top of the hat until the brim turns up slightly. Put the smaller bowl back, if necessary.

8 Allow the hat to dry thoroughly. Trim the edges of the brim. If you want a wider brim, glue pieces of cornhusk to the inside of the hat. If you want a narrower brim, just trim the edges more. Decorate the hat with a feather or whatever you'd like for a stylish look.

Angel Ornament medium

Probably the most common toy among the Native American people of the American Southwest was a cornhusk doll. This one has been turned into an angel to hang as a decoration.

continued →

Angel Ornament

You will need:

old sheet or towel

6 or 7 cornhusks

pan of water

paper towels

scissors

several strands of raffia

small ball of Spanish moss or a 1-inch Styrofoam ball

hot glue gun and glue sticks or craft glue (see Glue Gun Caution! on page 7)

corn silk, yarn, or embroidery thread

pencil or marker (optional)

How to do it:

1 Cover your work area with a sheet or towel. Soak the cornhusks in the water for 3 to 4 minutes. Remove them and dry on paper towels.

2 Cut a piece of cornhusk about 6 inches long. Tie a piece of raffia in the middle of it. Cut the ends of the raffia.

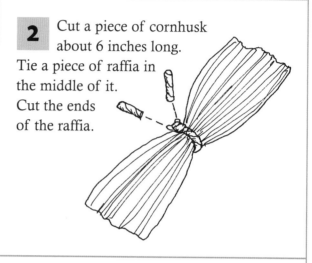

3 Place the center of the tied cornhusk on the top of the ball of moss. Gently spread out the front and back of the husk so it completely covers the ball. Tie a long piece of raffia under the chin to make a neck. Allow the long ends of the raffia to extend out on the sides for arms.

4 Take two or three long pieces of cornhusk and fold over the narrow top ends. Place the folded edges just under the head, one in the front, one in the back, and more on the sides, if necessary. Tie the cornhusks at the waist with a piece of raffia.

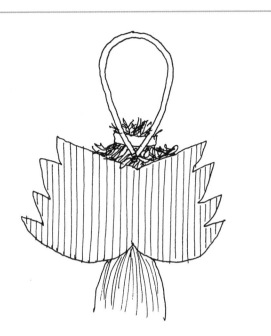

6 Make a small loop from a piece of raffia, tie it, then glue it to the back of the head so you can hang the ornament on your tree or elsewhere in your home. Make sure you let the glue dry completely before you try to hang it. Draw on a face with pencil or markers, if desired.

5 Cut wings from another piece of cornhusk. Glue in place in the back. Use corn silk, yarn, or embroidery thread to make the hair. Glue it in place. Make a halo by tying a piece of raffia into a circle, then glue it in place. Glue the hands together.

To make a doll instead of an ornament, don't glue on wings or a loop in the back. Try dressing the doll with a skirt and blouse made from dyed cornhusks (see pages 122–126). You could also make a bundle of dried flowers and place it in the doll's hands (see Drying Flowers on pages 148–149 and Dried-Flower Bouquet on page 150).

Bean Mosaic medium

You use the same technique for this project as you do for making the sand painting (see pages 89–91), but instead of colored sand, you'll glue down beans and seeds. Start collecting all kinds of seeds, nuts, and beans from the fruits you eat and the trees and flowers outside. If you need other kinds, or just more, you can always buy dried beans and seeds. Red beans, black beans, green split peas, and sunflower seeds with the husks still on are available at supermarkets and are very inexpensive.

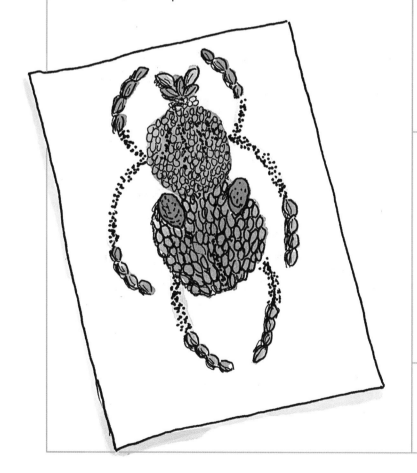

old sheet or towel

pencil

heavy paper or poster board, cut to the size you want

variety of seeds, beans, nuts, and pits

craft glue

paintbrush

spoon, if needed

How to do it:

1 Cover your work area with a sheet or towel. With the pencil, draw a design on the paper. Figure out which seeds and beans you want to use to fill different parts of the design.

2 Work one part of the design at a time. Spread on the glue with a paintbrush, then sprinkle on the seeds or beans. If the seeds are very small, place them on a spoon and tap the edge of the spoon to drop them. Keep working until the design is covered with the nuts and seeds.

3 Allow the glue to dry thoroughly. Shake off extra seeds.

Seed Packets *easy*

Everything a plant needs for starting a new life is found in its seed. Not all plants put out seeds that are easy to collect, but many garden flowers do. The plants you grow from these seeds may not look exactly like their parents, but you'll have fun anyway. Try collecting seeds from aster, black-eyed Susan, butterfly weed, chrysanthemum, cosmos, milkweed, sunflower, and zinnia. Gather the seeds, separate them from their pods and any extra material, and decorate envelopes for seed packets.

COSMOS seeds

MARIGOLD seeds

ZINNIA seeds

You will need:

plants and flowers with seedpods

paper

envelopes

pencil or pen

materials and tools for pressing or hammering plants (see pages 160–161, and 106–109, optional)

index card or construction paper

markers

craft glue

How to do it:

1 Watch the plants closely as the blooms turn to seedpods. Wait until they are dry and crisp, then pick a pod and open it gently. If the seeds are soft and green, wait a few days and try again. The seeds must be brown and dry.

2 Spread out the contents of the seedpod on a piece of paper and separate the seeds from the rest of the stuff. Put the seeds into an envelope and write the kind of seed on the back. Decorate the envelope with one of the Art Skills you've learned from this book (such as pressing or hammering plants; see pages 160–161, and 106–109, respectively). In either case, decorate a small card with markers and glue the illustration to the front of the envelope. Be sure to include the name of the plant on the front.

Cantaloupe Seed Necklace medium

You won't believe how beautiful this is! If you don't want to string the entire necklace with seeds, do just the center part, then tie leather lacing to the ends. Or alternate the cantaloupe seeds with beads or other seeds. The big advantage of using melon seeds is that they are soft enough to pierce with a needle. *Note:* This project is a little time-consuming, but it makes a wonderful gift. For a shorter project, string only 8 to 9 inches of seeds and tie the ends securely to the leather lacing to finish the necklace.

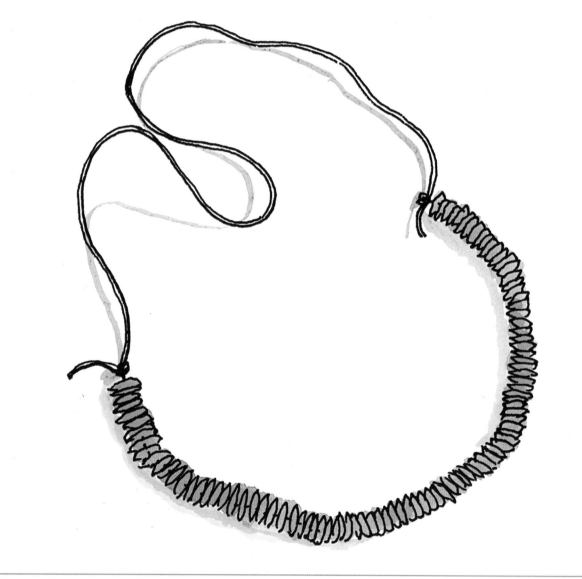

You will need:

1 cantaloupe (or watermelon) cut open

colander

baking sheet

bowl

clear fishing line, 24–30 inches long

needle with a large eye

black or brown leather lacing (optional)

How to do it:

1 In the sink, use your hands to scoop out the seeds and pulp from the cantaloupe and put them into the colander. Run water over the seeds and pulp, separating the seeds from the pulp with your fingers.

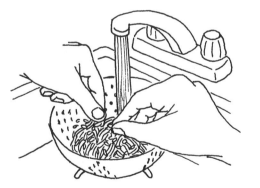

2 When you have separated them as much as you can, place the seeds on a baking sheet in the sunshine to dry for a couple of hours. This makes it much easier to finish cleaning them. When the seeds are dry, scrape off any extra pulp with your fingers. Place the seeds in a bowl.

3 Thread the fishing line through the needle and tie a knot at one end.

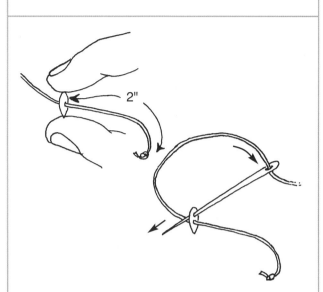

4 Leaving the seeds in the bowl, pierce one with the needle, then pull it down the needle and onto the fishing line. Push it carefully toward the end, leaving a tail about 2 inches. Push the needle back through the seed (but not through the same hole!), pulling the line tight and securing the seed at the end of the fishing line. This gives you an anchor so the rest of the seeds won't slip off the end.

5 Continue to pierce the seeds and pull them across the needle and onto the line until you have a pretty string of seeds. Tie the ends of the string to the leather lacing if you want the necklace to be longer.

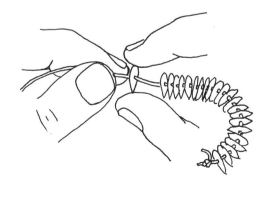

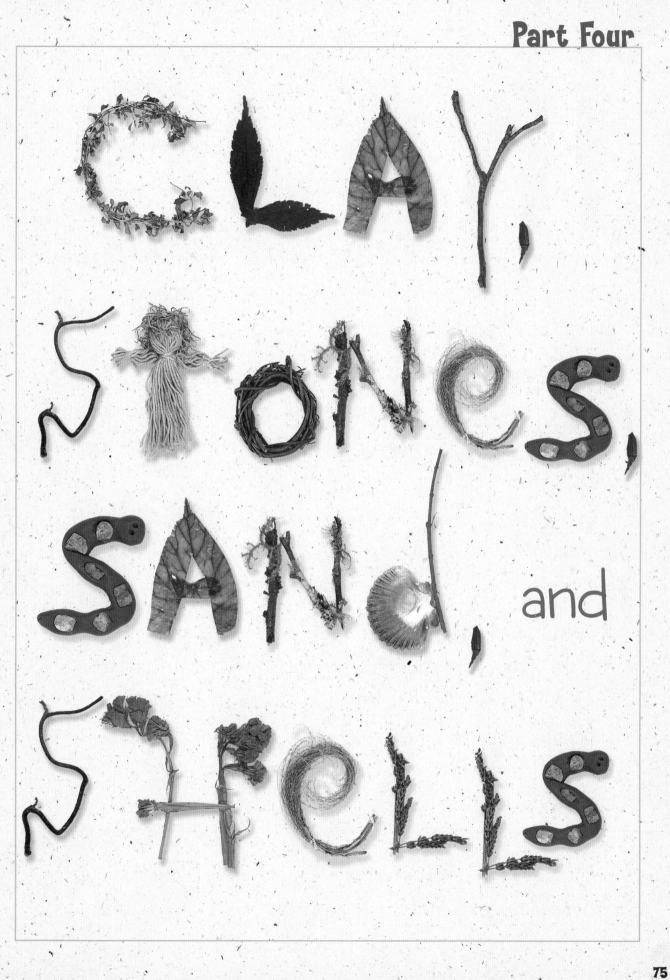

Part Four

CLAY, STONES, SAND, and SHELLS

ost of the materials we use for nature crafts are from once-living organisms — but not all. Many beautiful things can be made from rocks, sand, soil, and shells, which are actually houses for sea creatures but aren't alive themselves. (*Note:* Some of the projects that call for shells also call for sea creatures, such as sea horses or sand dollars that have died a natural death.)

Using Clay in Art

In the southwestern United States, native peoples baked clay into adobe bricks to make houses. Clay is also used to make pots and jewelry. No matter where you live, you can find soil with enough clay in it to make your own pots. You can also purchase clay at a craft store, making it possible to do ancient crafts with the convenience of modern materials.

Stones for Art

Stones have been important to people of different cultures throughout the ages. Some stones, such as diamonds, are extremely valuable. Other stones are as commonplace as soil. Wherever people live, though, they appreciate beautiful stones. Whether they are shiny because they have been pounded by water in a river for thousands of years or have been cut and polished by a machine, smooth, glossy stones display beautiful colors and patterns.

Native Americans of the Southwest first used turquoise and shells to make jewelry. Although they were able to find turquoise fairly easily near their homeland, the tribes of New Mexico and Arizona had to travel or trade to obtain shells. This made their jewelry even more valuable.

Beachcombing

Oceans cover about 72 percent of the earth's surface, and that water is teeming with life. What lives in or near a particular seashore depends on the climate, weather, changes in temperature, and nature of the shore — whether it is rocky, sandy, or muddy. Some shores and beaches are full of shells; others are almost barren.

No matter what kinds of shells or sea creatures you find and where you find them, make sure you are not harming a living animal by removing it from the ocean. You don't want to take someone's house, especially if he or she is still inside! (Look in the hole; if it is solid and not hollow, the creature is still inside.) Check to make sure that a sand dollar, starfish, or sea horse is not still alive. If it is bleached white and brittle, it is not alive. If it is alive, throw it back into the ocean.

STONE SYMBOLISM

Many stones have special symbolism, or meaning, attached to them. Some of these include:

AMBER: Protection

BLACK AGATE: Courage, prosperity, and vigor

GARNET: Clear thoughts

GOLD: Divine illumination

MALACHITE: Health and good fortune

PEARL: Strength and patience

TIGER EYE: Inner strength

TURQUOISE: Safe travel

Making Pottery Clay

An Egyptian legend holds that the earth was formed when the god Ptah shaped it on a potter's wheel. Even if you don't believe this story, it's true that potters have been creating objects of usefulness and beauty almost since the beginning of recorded history. Clay is found almost everywhere on earth, and people quickly learned to mix this special dirt with water and mold it, then bake it to make bowls, jugs, and vases.

Just like many other things that were originally made for practical purposes, clay and pots were soon made into pieces of art as well. Much of the earthenware found from ancient times is beautiful, with intricate designs and bright colors.

Clay is found everywhere on earth, and it's easy to make it into pottery clay. The best place to look is in a stream along a riverbank, or beside a lake. There may even be some in your own backyard.

You will need:

old sheet or towel

1 cup clay soil

screen or wire sifter

small bowl

water, if needed

⅛ cup sand or crushed shells

clean paper

airtight container

How to do it:

1 Cover your work area with a sheet or towel. Place the clay soil on the screen and set it over the bowl.

2 Rub the soil back and forth until pieces comes through the screen. Wipe the bottom of the screen occasionally, as soil tends to collect there. Discard the rocks, pebbles, and other debris that will not go through the screen.

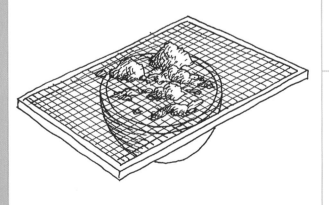

3 Push enough soil through the screen to make a handful of clay.

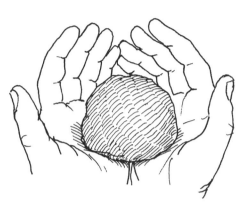

4 Gather the clay in your hands and make a ball. If it won't stick together, add a drop or two of water. Mix in the sand or crushed shells and more water, if needed.

5 Roll the clay in your hands and squish it out onto clean paper, then gather it back in your hands. Roll the clay, squish it, and gather it back again and again until it is soft and easy to work.

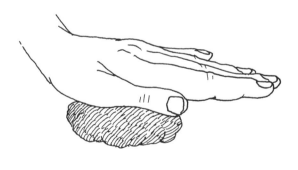

6 Store the clay in an airtight container until you're ready to use it.

Clay Pot *easy*

Most potters bake their clay in a very hot oven called a *kiln*. But you can bake your pot in a regular oven (don't use a microwave!). The pot may crack and it may not hold water, but you can use it for jewelry, pens, or anything else. Just don't eat or drink out of it. (This project requires adult supervision.)

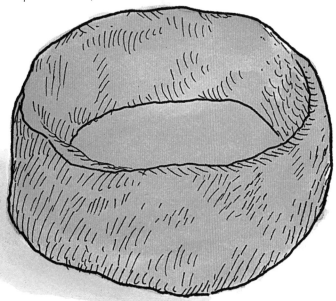

How to do it:

1 Cover your work area with a sheet or towel. Preheat the oven to 400°F.

2 Use your thumbs to push in the center of the ball of clay and begin the pot. As you push in, build up the sides, smoothing them with your fingers. Try to make the walls even in height and thickness. Add drops of water as needed. Keep the clay moist so that it won't crack as you work.

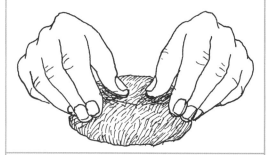

3 When your pot is nicely shaped, place it on a piece of foil on a baking sheet and bake until it is dry and hard. Small pots take 15–20 minutes. Don't over-bake it or the pot will crack.

FIRED POTS

When clay is exposed to enough heat, it dries out and hardens and will keep its shape. The first pots were simply baked by the heat of the sun, but soon it was discovered that putting the pots into a fire brought better results.

Working with Polymer Clay

Polymer clay is much easier to use than homemade clay, because it doesn't dry out. It stays soft until you heat it in the oven. There are a few tools that will come in handy. Use a wooden skewer to poke holes through the clay or to draw designs in it before you bake it. A plastic knife helps cut the clay, giving you a clean edge. Use a smooth plastic ruler to push the clay against and create a flat surface. A safety pin is good for cutting or pushing very small areas. Here are some other guidelines:

⊚ Keep your work area clean. Clay picks up dirt and dust, pet hairs, and other unwanted items.

⊚ The clay bakes exactly as you form it. If you have rough edges or an uneven surface, it will bake right in.

⊚ You may place things (such as stones) in the clay before you bake it. If they fall out after you remove the piece from the oven, use a drop of glue to place it where you want it.

⊚ To join two colors, lay one on top of the other and push gently so they stick. Don't smoosh them together or the colors will blend.

⊚ If you want, paint baked clay items with a shiny glaze to protect them from dirt and scratches.

BAKING POLYMER CLAY

You can bake polymer clay in a regular oven or a toaster oven. Preheat the oven to 275°F and set the clay pieces on aluminum foil, in a pan, or on a baking sheet you will not be using for food. It's important to keep clay equipment separate from food equipment.

A good rule is to bake the clay for 15–20 minutes per $\frac{1}{4}$ inch of thickness. Don't burn or overcook it, or the clay will turn colors and become brittle.

African Necklace *easy*

These look like funny-shaped dice. Strung onto a piece of leather or twine, these necklaces were worn by African men. They make great projects for a birthday party or gifts for your friends. (This project requires adult supervision.)

You will need:

old sheet or towel

polymer clay in two colors

wooden skewer

twine or leather about 16 inches long

scissors

How to do it:

1 Cover your work area with a sheet or towel. Preheat the oven to 275°F.

2 Mold a very small ball of clay into a long oblong shape, a little narrower at the top than at the bottom. Decorate one side with several small circles of a different-colored clay, like dots on a pair of dice. Push a wooden skewer cross-wise through the top to create a hole. Repeat until you have three to five pieces.

3 Bake according to the instructions in the box "Baking Polymer Clay" on page 81.

4 Thread the twine or leather through the pieces to make a necklace. Decide how long you want the necklace to be (make sure it can slip over your head easily), then tie a knot in the twine and cut the ends with scissors.

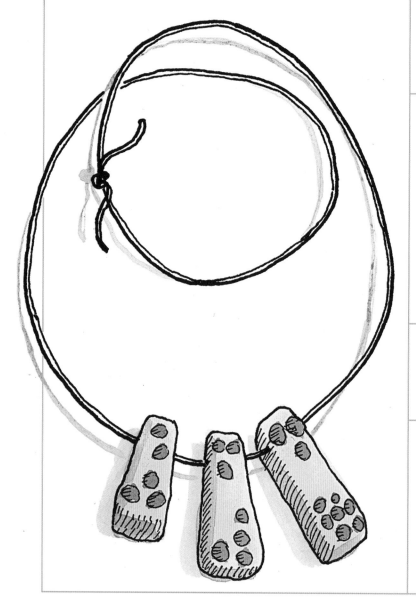

ANIMAL FETISHES

A fetish is a small carved object that represents a particular animal. Native peoples believed (and still do) that each animal has desirable qualities and characteristics. It was thought that wearing or carrying a fetish of an animal would be a constant reminder of its important traits.

Fetishes were especially important to some of the southwestern Native American tribes. The Zuni became famous for their small animal creations. Although traditionally their fetishes were carved out of stone, you can mold yours from clay. You're only making a copy, though. Only people who have carefully studied the culture and customs of those who originally created them can make true fetishes.

If you don't want to make your own clay, you can always do any of these clay crafts using store-bought products. If you choose to use a polymer clay, such as Fimo or Sculpey, you can simply bake it in an oven. In addition, polymer clay comes in a wide range of colors. Don't buy modeling clay or artist's clay for these projects; those products tend to dry out quickly, and the finished items must be fired in a kiln.

Animal symbolism from the Zuni of the American Southwest

- **BEAR: Strength, healing, introspection**
- **BUFFALO: Power, strength, abundance**
- **BUTTERFLY: Beauty, balance, transformation**
- **COYOTE: Teaching, humor**
- **DEER: Agility, speed, gentleness**
- **EAGLE: Illumination, vision, clarity**
- **HAWK: Nobility, inspiration, energy**
- **HORSE: Courage, speed, safe journey**
- **HUMMINGBIRD: Joy, beauty, thankfulness**
- **LIZARD: Wisdom, silence**
- **TURTLE: Longevity, loyalty, peace**
- **WOLF: Commitment, sociability, stamina**

Polymer Clay Fetishes *easy*

A fetish can be any size you want. Traditionally, they were rather small (the size of charms) and were worn as necklaces. *Note:* If you don't feel confident about shaping your own animals, roll out the clay like cookie dough and cut it with small cookie cutters in the shapes of animals. (This project requires adult supervision.)

How to make a thunderbird:

Preheat the oven to 275°F. Roll a medium-sized ball of clay between your palms to make a rounded log about 2 inches long. Curve the top to one side for a beak. Push out the bottom into a triangle. Roll out a smaller ball of clay into a log about 2 inches long but thinner than the first log. Place this across the back of the bird's body to make the wings. Make marks on the clay with a wooden skewer or make small dots for the eyes and decorations out of a different-colored clay.

Bake according to the instructions on page 81. Remove from the oven, let cool.

How to make a lizard:

Preheat the oven to 275°F. Roll a small ball of clay into a log about 3 inches long. Roll two smaller balls of clay into thin logs about 2 inches long. Push out the head into a triangular shape and thin out the tail into a nice long curve. Place one thin log across the body about

1 inch from the top (for the arms) and the next one about 2 inches down the body (for the legs). Bend them a little bit for "elbows" and "knees" and use a safety pin to etch in some fingers and toes. Make eyes and decorate as you wish.

Bake according to the instructions on page 81. Remove from the oven, let cool.

How to make a bear:

Preheat the oven to 275°F. Form a small ball of clay into a rectangle about 1½ inches long. Use your finger or the side of a pencil to push up from the bottom in the center. This will cause the top to round over — just like a bear's back! It will also help create legs. Make the nose a little longer and pinch in the legs to make them thinner. Make a tiny turquoise arrow and press it onto the bear.

Bake according to the instructions on page 81. Remove from the oven, let cool.

FINISHING TOUCHES

If you wish to wear a fetish as a necklace, be sure to add a loop at the top or push a hole through the top of the fetish with a wooden skewer before you bake it so you'll have something for the string to go through.

Thread a piece of string, ribbon, or leather through the hole. Decide how long you want the necklace to be, then tie a knot in the string and cut the ends with scissors.

Animal Stones *easy*

Pretty stones have always been used for a variety of artistic purposes, particularly carving. Many artists believed that stones had spirits within them that wanted to come out in different shapes and forms. It was the job of the artist to help a spirit shape come out through carving. Often special smaller stones were tied together almost like a medicine or amulet bag (see pages 131–133) and tied to the back of the carved animal for extra luck or good fortune.

If you look hard enough at the stones around you, you'll notice that some of them do seem to look like animals. Collect some stones that have animal shapes. They don't have to look exactly like any animal. If a stone just reminds you of a buffalo or a fish or a horse or anything else, that's all that's necessary.

You will need:

old sheet or towel

animal-shaped stones

polymer clay, if needed

small colorful or special stones

thin pieces of raffia

hot glue gun and glue sticks or craft glue, if needed (see Glue Gun Caution! on page 7)

TURQUOISE

Turquoise held much symbolism for Native Americans. It was a symbol of sky and water and was associated with healing and protection. The Navajo presented turquoise bracelets to newborns to keep them safe from accidents and diseases. Turquoise was considered good luck and was given to travelers to protect them on their journeys.

How to do it:

1 Cover your work area with a sheet or towel. Select an animal-shaped stone from your collection.

2 If this stone doesn't stand up by itself, make a small clay stand for it (see page 29).

3 Pick out some colorful or special stones. These should be small enough to fit easily on the back of your animal-shaped stone. (You can always purchase polished, colorful stones at a craft store or rock shop.)

4 To make a stone bag, tie the small stones together with a very thin piece of raffia. Put a dot of glue onto the raffia to keep it from slipping off the stones, if necessary. Tie or glue the stones to the animal-shaped stone.

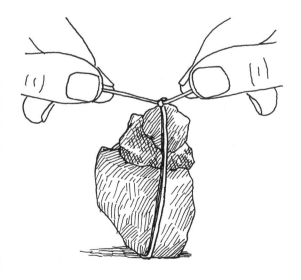

Painted Stones *easy*

Painting on stones or stone walls was one of the first expressions of art by native peoples. Although you can make your own paints (see pages 138–139), you can also use store-bought paint to create your own piece of "prehistoric" rock art.

You will need:

old sheet or towel

flat, light-colored stone

soap and water

pencil

acrylic paints

small paintbrush

How to do it:

Cover your work area with a sheet or towel. Clean the stone with soap and water.

Draw a design on the stone with a pencil (use the designs shown here, find others, or create your own). Paint the design on the rock.

Remember that this is supposed to look primitive!

Sand Painting *challenging*

A sacred tradition of the Navajo tribe was sand painting. These "paintings" were created out of colored sand, cornmeal, pollen, and ground stones or bark. They were made by a medicine man and his assistants, then used to help heal a sick person. Each grain of sand, each color used, each line drawn was symbolic. When you make one of these, remember that it is only a replica. Be respectful of the true traditional sand paintings of the Navajo people.

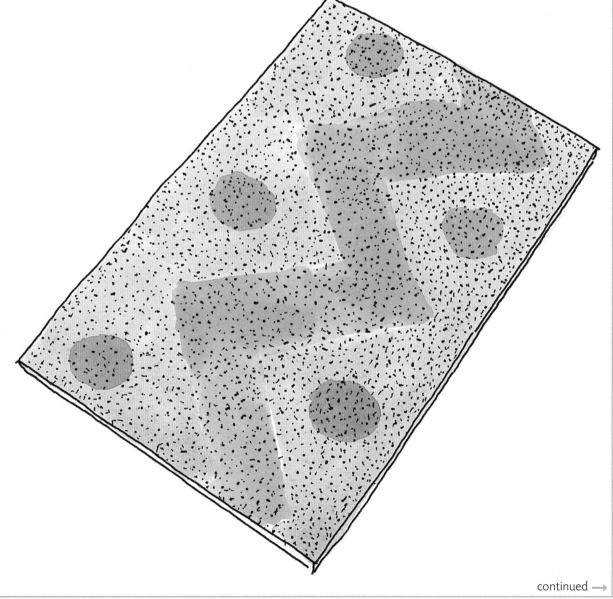

continued ⟶

Sand Painting

You will need:

old sheet or towel

design

pencil

stiff paper, such as poster board

3 colors of sand or white sand, food coloring (blue, green, yellow, and red), measuring cup, and wooden or plastic spoons

3 small bowls

paintbrush

craft glue

old newspapers

envelope

SAND COLORS

Sand comes naturally in many colors and shades, including white, yellow, gray, black, brown, and red. Every time you go to the beach, collect a little sand to take home with you. See how many kinds of sand you can gather. If you have only white sand, you can color it with food coloring. It's fast and easy.

How to do it:

1 Cover your work area with a sheet or towel. Choose a small, simple design. Try the one here or make up your own. *Hint:* Straight lines are easier to drop color in than curves.

2 Draw your design on the paper and decide what color you want for each part of the design.

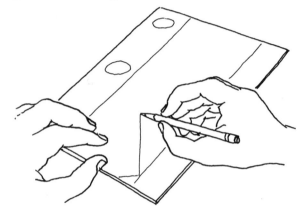

3 If you are using naturally colored sand, place the colors in separate bowls. If you need to color the sand, place about ¼ cup of white sand in a bowl and add several drops of the desired food coloring, mixing well with a spoon. Mix one color at a time and use a different bowl and spoon for each color.

4 Choose one part of the design to work with — for example, the zigzag pattern. Use the paintbrush to brush glue all over that part of the design. Do this carefully and make sure that you have painted right up to the lines *but not over them.*

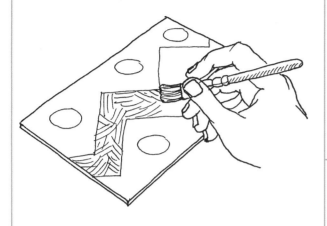

5 Quickly, before the glue dries, sprinkle the desired color sand over the places you have put glue. The sand will stick immediately. Don't worry if the sand is piled too thick; you can shake off the excess. Make sure that you have put on enough sand to cover the design.

6 After a couple of minutes, turn the paper upside down over a piece of newspaper and gently tap the edges to get rid of excess sand.

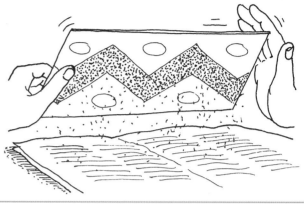

7 Let the first color dry completely. Choose another color for another part of the design, paint glue over that part, and sprinkle on the sand. You'll have to be more careful this time to avoid getting sand on the parts you've already colored. For a smooth, clean line, place an envelope along the edge of the design to protect parts of it that you have already colored.

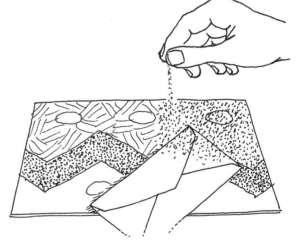

8 After a couple of minutes, turn the paper upside down over a piece of newspaper and gently tap the edges to get rid of excess sand. Continue until all parts of the design are covered with colored sand. Tap off any excess.

Zen Garden *easy*

The beauty of sand means something completely different to the Japanese. With their appreciation of simplicity, they believe that sand raked with lines is beautiful. Entire gardens exist with nothing more than raked sand and artfully placed rocks, and sometimes a tree or shrub. These are called Zen gardens and are created to give visitors a sense of tranquillity.

You may not have a space outside for a large Japanese garden, but you can create a mini landscape that is just right for a desk or table. This one consists of sand and a few rocks. You'll need a rake, too, so that you can rake the sand into patterns you find pleasing.

You will need:

old sheet or towel

acrylic "box" picture frame with sides about 2 inches deep

bag of clean sand (sifted, if necessary)

3 beautiful stones — not too big, and different shapes and sizes

several small twigs

hot glue gun and glue sticks or craft glue (see Glue Gun Caution! on page 7)

THE ART OF SIMPLICITY

While creating this garden, remember the Japanese word *shibusa,* which means "restraint, good taste, and elegant simplicity." Although you could stick a dozen rocks and some cactus and dried flowers into your Zen garden, its real beauty is in its simplicity. Allow the shapes of the rocks, the shadows cast by the sun, and the lines created by the rake to be the only decoration.

How to do it:

1 Cover your work area with a sheet or towel. Empty the frame and turn it upside down so you have a clear acrylic box. Put the sand in the frame.

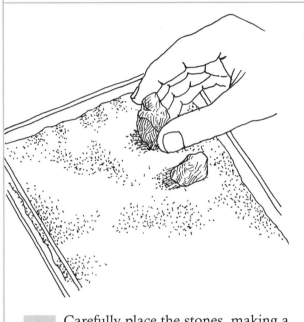

2 Carefully place the stones, making a grouping in one corner.

3 To make the twig rake, break five thin twigs all the same length. Glue four of them, evenly spaced, to the fifth twig (the crosspiece), allowing most of each twig to extend outward.

4 Glue the cross-piece (with the thin twigs attached) to a longer twig; this will be the handle.

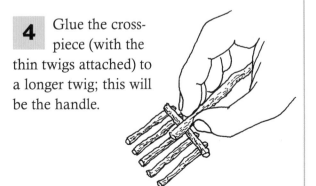

Shell Buttons *easy*

It's fun to use shells as buttons on shirts, jackets, or bags, but it's hard to get them sewn on unless you try the easy trick in this project.

Shells come in all shapes and sizes, so you can find ones to fit your clothes — no matter what shape or size you are!

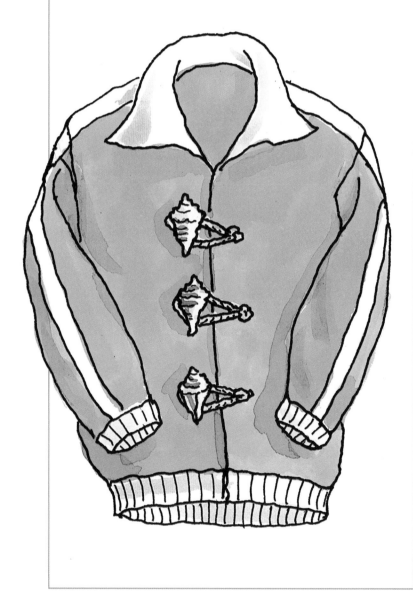

You will need:

old newspapers

hot glue gun and glue sticks or craft glue (see Glue Gun Caution! on page 7)

small wooden beads with a hole through them

small, interestingly shaped seashells

needle and thread

twine or hand-dyed cotton string

How to do it:

1 Cover your work area with newspaper. Glue a bead to the back of each shell so that the holes are exposed.

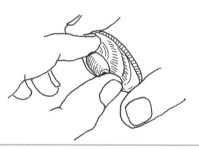

2 Let the glue dry, then sew the bead onto the front of a shirt, jacket, or bag.

3 To secure the shell button, cut a loop of twine or string large enough to slip over the shell easily. Sew the twine opposite the button so that when the twine loops over the shell, it brings together the two sides.

Shell Neck Piece medium

A very handsome replica of a Native American shell neck piece can be made with shells, wooden beads, and leather lacing. If you want, make two rows, tying more lacing and more shells underneath the first, for a double strand. Just make sure the holes in the beads are large enough to string lacing through.

continued ➞

Shell Neck Piece

You will need:

old sheet or towel

several small to medium-sized shells (choose the best-looking ones)

thin lacing 18–24 inches long

hot glue gun and glue sticks or craft glue (see Glue Gun Caution! on page 7)

wooden beads with holes through them

THE VALUE OF SHELLS

Shells were important to many native peoples. They used them for containers, ornaments, and musical instruments. Several tribes made beads, called *wampum*, from clamshells. These were woven into belts, which were considered quite valuable and were used in both trade and ceremonies. Pretty little shells called *cowries* were traded and used as money in many African nations.

How to do it:

1 Cover your work area with a sheet or towel. Lay out your shells in a pleasing way. The largest, showiest shell should be in the center. The shells on either side of the showiest one should get increasingly smaller as they approach the back.

2 Cut a piece of lacing long enough to slip easily over your head when tied into a loop. Untie it so that it is a straight piece. Make sure it will go through the holes in the beads.

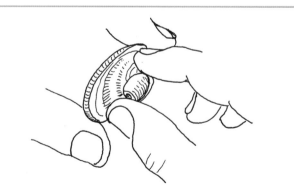

3 Glue a bead to the back of each shell so the holes are exposed. Let the glue dry. Keep the shells in the order you want them on the neckpiece.

4 Thread the lacing through the first bead, leaving a tail about 4 inches. Tie a knot on the other side of the bead to secure the shell in place.

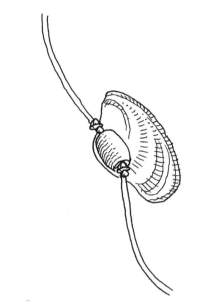

5 Thread the lacing through the next bead. Place the shell where you want it and tie a knot on the other side of the bead to secure the shell in place.

6 Continue to thread the lacing through each bead, tying knots so that the shells will stay on the lacing where you want them.

7 When all the beads have been threaded through the lacing and tied in place, tie the ends of the lacing together.

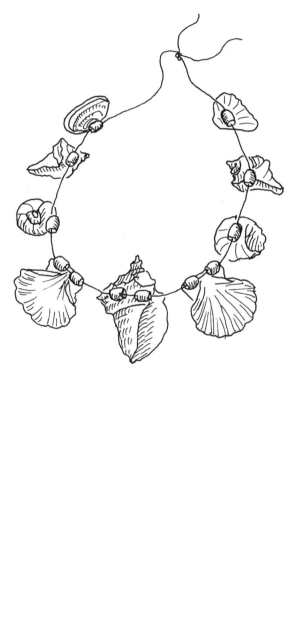

Shell Candles challenging

You can put candles in all kinds of containers, but the most beautiful are those you find in nature. Pouring hot wax into an empty shell makes a stunning candle, but be very careful — hot wax can catch fire easily! (This project requires adult supervision.)

You will need:

old pieces of candle or paraffin wax

8-ounce can (such as from canned vegetables or soup)

medium-sized saucepan

candlewicking (sold at craft stores)

several large shells with open cavities

oven mitt

several drops of your favorite fragrance oil (optional)

How to do it:

1 Make sure the candle pieces are clean. Set the can in a saucepan of water and turn the heat on low. Place the candle pieces in the can. Heat until the wax has melted. How quickly this happens depends on how much wax you have, but it shouldn't take more than a few minutes. *Caution:* Wax catches fire very easily.

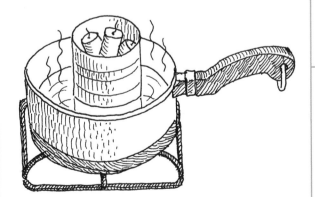

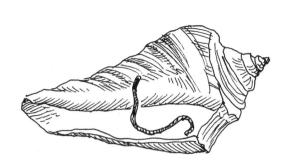

2 Cut a small length of candlewicking that fits into the cavity in each shell and extends upward about ½ inch or so. Don't worry if the wicking won't stand up straight; the wax will help it do so as it hardens.

3 Using the oven mitt, carefully pick up the can of melted wax. Holding on to the wicking with one hand, carefully pour hot wax into the candle cavity until it is full. Hold the wick for a few minutes until the wax has hardened a little.

4 Repeat with the other shells. Scent your candles by adding a drop or two of fragrance oil to each one just after pouring, if desired.

Shell Candles **99**

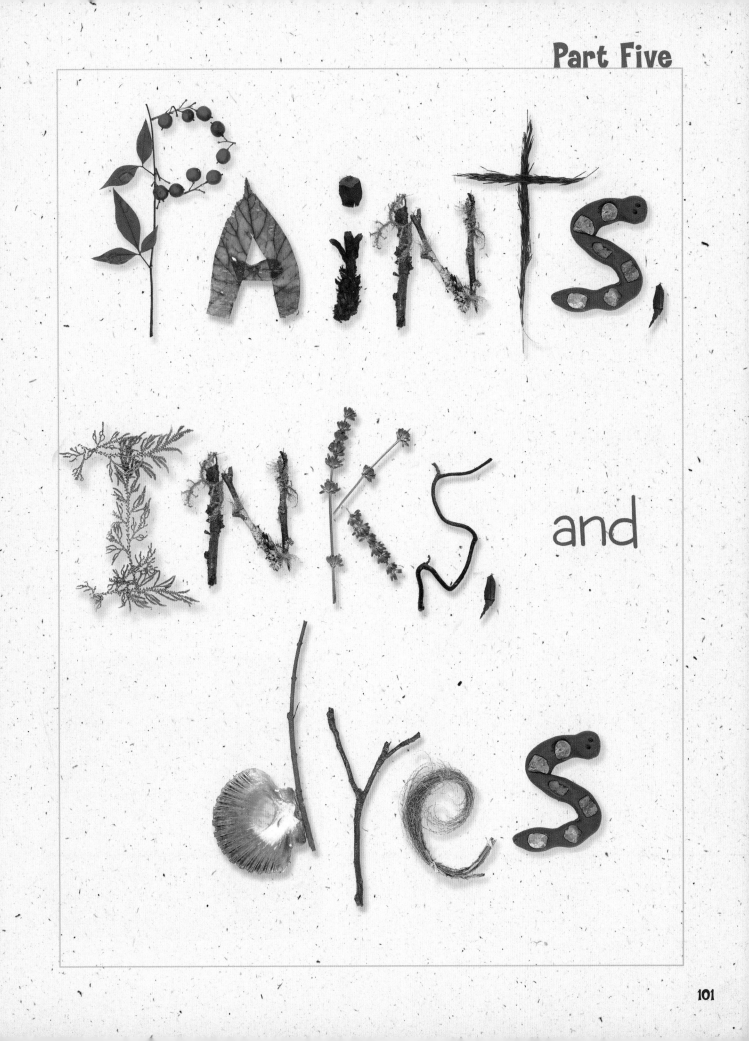

Part Five

Paints, Inks, and dyes

Imagine what a dreary place the world would be without color. Color is exciting and it's everywhere, especially in nature. Even the earliest artists who painted on cave walls learned how to make colorful paints just by grinding red and yellow rocks.

Soon people not only wanted to look at color in art, but also wanted to wear it. So as civilizations developed, people began searching for things that would color and brighten their clothes. Any material, extracted from all kinds of things but used specifically to color cloth and paper, is called a *dye*.

Colors to Dye For

Where did they look for dyes? In nature, of course. Although nature is full of colors (think about a rainbow or fall foliage!), not everything that is brightly colored can be used for coloring *things*. Even materials that look as though they would be good for coloring cloth, such as beautifully colored fall leaves, don't always work. (If you try to use bright red maple leaves to color cloth, for example, you won't have much success, because the leaves are too dry to release pigment.)

IN THE LABORATORY

The first synthetic (or man-made) dye was created when a scientist in England, W. H. Perkin, was experimenting with making a medicine to cure malaria. When he mixed together two chemicals in the laboratory, the solution turned a bright purplish red, which turned out to be a wonderful, long-lasting dye.

Another problem was that even when people did find materials that colored cloth, the vibrant shades did not last very long. Some colors faded away after a few hours in the sunlight and some came out when they got wet.

The search went on. Early artists probably tried all kinds of things, but after years of experimenting, they had the best luck with certain types of rocks and soils, certain colorful plants, seashells, and even insects. For example, a small bug called a cochineal, from Central America, makes a great red.

Making Brighter Dyes

It was clear from the very beginning that the brighter the dye, the better people liked it and the more valuable it was. Fifteen thousand years ago, the Egyptians were making blue dye from the indigo plant and red dye from the madder plant and then selling them. These plants still produce some of the brightest natural colors.

Among the ancient Greeks, purple was the most precious color. Sailors knew that a mollusk (called *murex*; plural, *murices*) found in the Mediterranean Sea lives in a long, spiral shell that opens at one end. A brilliant purple dye was made from mucus taken from the glands of this shellfish. It took a lot of murices and a long time to extract the dye: about 12,000 murices produced only 1 gram of dye! This made purple dye very valuable, and purple became the color for kings.

Early artists found that plants offered bright and beautiful colors. Saffron, which is made from the crocus flower, makes a golden color. The Europeans made colors from oak bark, walnut shells, pomegranate flowers, and lichens. Although today most dyes are made from chemicals, some are still made from these natural elements.

Making Paint

Artists used similar natural materials to make paints that they could apply with a brush. In painting, though, not only the color was important but also the consistency — that is, how easily the substance flowed off the brush. Think about painting with peanut butter, then think about painting with grape juice. Do you see the problems? The first is too thick to spread easily; the second is too thin to cover well. Something in between is needed.

When artists discovered how to mix colors with something either slimy or sticky (called a *binder*), the paints lasted much longer and were easier to apply. They found that the best binders were egg whites, the sap from the gum tree, gelatin (such as Jell-O), and beeswax. Recipes for different paints were closely guarded secrets and the recipes themselves became valuable. (See pages 138–139 for making your own paint.)

Making Colors That Won't Fade

No matter where a color came from, the goal of those who made dyes and paints was to make colors that would not fade in the sun or wash out easily. This is the same challenge we face today when we color things from nature. As you explore the wonderful world of creating dyes, paint, and colors with the materials you find in nature, remember that even when you use the best materials, the brightness will fade and water will wash out much of the color. But that's part of the experience of using art supplies from nature. Nothing in nature stays the same, for everything is alive and growing and changing. The brightest colors in the garden are going to fade and eventually die. The brilliant leaves of fall will drop off and turn to dust. A sunset showing brilliant colors lasts only a few minutes.

> ### BUGS FOR ART
>
> The Greeks found that they could get beautiful colors from the dried bodies of a scale insect called kermes. The insect lives on oak trees in the Mediterranean region. This dye was also very expensive, because it required a lot of time and effort to extract the color.

When you "borrow" colors from nature, know that they will not stay bright forever, but nothing man-made can compare to the beauty of these natural colors. Create and enjoy, and know that nature is generous with her colors and that tomorrow you can dye and paint and color again, just as tomorrow there will be another sunrise and another blue sky.

Hammering on Paper

Every once in a while, nature offers a package deal. That's what happens when you hammer plants. Not only do you get great colors, but you also get the details that make plants so beautiful.

Hammering is full of surprises. Many of the plants change colors when you hammer them. Not all plants are good for hammering (for example, white flowers will not hammer). Just experiment (and remember to make notes) to determine which plants work best for you. Good hammering plants include carrot tops, coreopsis, cosmos, dianthus, dill, fern, common geranium, impatiens, lobelia, maple leaves, and vinca. Look them up in Nature Skills, starting on page 203. When hammering flowers, select small, flat blossoms that do *not* have a thick center or layers of petals. (This project requires adult supervision.)

CHOOSING PLANTS

- **Select flat blossoms that don't have layers of petals.**

- **Choose flowers that have thin, brightly colored petals.**

- **Don't choose plants that have hard or fleshy centers.**

- **Don't choose leaves that are shiny or waxy.**

- **Choose plants that are completely dry, or use a paper towel to blot up any moisture.**

- **Don't choose plants with thick or fleshy veins or leaves.**

You will need:

smooth board (such as a clipboard or a chopping board)

old newspapers or magazines

paper towels

white construction paper

flowers, small and brightly colored

removable adhesive tape (available at office or art supply stores)

hammer

iron

How to do it:

1 Set the board on top of a stack of newspapers (to help dull the noise). Place a paper towel on top of the board.

2 Put the construction paper on top of the paper towel. Place a flower on this, colorful side down. Completely cover the plant with *removable* tape or tape the edges and cover the rest with another paper towel.

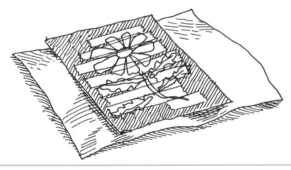

3 Hold the hammer near the head and tap gently all over. Plants change colors as you do this, so make sure you've hammered everything. If using a top paper towel, pigment will bleed through, showing where you've hammered (but not taped areas).

4 When you've hammered the entire plant, leave the plant taped on, then use a warm (not hot) iron to press the paper on the *back* to heat-set the colors. Do not iron directly on the tape, as it will melt. Press for 20 seconds.

5 Turn over the paper and carefully peel off the tape — the plant material should come off, too. Carefully scrape away any leftover plant from the paper.

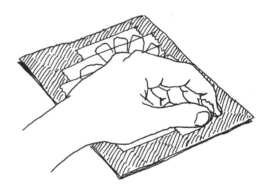

6 Practice some more, using different plants, then try one of the projects starting on page 111.

Hammering on Cloth

Many plants hammer better on cloth than they do on paper (most leaves fall into this category). Follow the directions for hammering on paper, but use regular adhesive tape instead of removable tape. Unfortunately, most hammered images fade when you wash them. Some, however, such as summer ferns, last a fairly long time. There are ways to make the images last forever, though. Either photocopy your masterpieces or scan them into a computer and print them on T-shirt transfer paper. People who dye cloth use something called a *mordant* to help the colors stay in longer. Treating cloth with a mordant also helps hammered colors stay bright. For directions on how to use a mordant, see page 123. (This project requires adult supervision.)

You will need:

smooth board (such as a clipboard or a chopping board)

old newspapers or magazines

paper towels

small pieces of white fabric about 4 inches square

flowers, small and brightly colored

removable adhesive tape (available at office or art supply stores)

hammer

iron

CREATING A GOOD DESIGN

You can make great designs with hammered images. Try hammering a flower or two, then hammer stems and add a couple of leaves. Be sure to practice hammering each plant on an extra piece of paper or fabric before you hammer on your "masterpiece." *Note:* The stems of most plants are full of moisture and don't hammer well. Practice until you find a stem that gives you a solid line, then use that whenever you need a stem. For a basic stem, a thin blade of grass will work well.

How to do it:

1 Follow steps 1 and 2 on page 107, substituting fabric for the construction paper. Once the plant is taped down, carefully turn over the cloth and hammer on the *back* of the fabric. The pigment should bleed through, showing where you've hammered. Be sure to hammer the entire plant.

2 Leave the plant taped on, then use a warm (not hot) iron to press the cloth on the *back* to heat-set the colors. Do not iron directly on the tape, as it will melt. Press for 20 seconds.

3 Turn over the cloth, peel away the tape, and scrape off any plant material still on the fabric.

TROUBLESHOOTING

If you're having trouble getting a clear image, here is a variety of tips and techniques:

- Hammer on cloth instead of paper. It's an easier technique.

- Use a different kind of plant. Some are just too squishy and splatter rather than give you crisp edges. If you have a squishy plant that you really want to hammer, try putting extra paper towels underneath and on top of it before you hammer. The paper towels should help absorb some of the moisture. Make notes so you'll remember which plants you have the most success with.

- Try the same plant in different seasons. Remember that you need to hammer just a small piece of leaf or flower to see if it's going to work; you don't have to hammer the whole thing.

- Make sure both the plant and the paper or cloth are completely dry before you hammer.

- Don't allow the tape to get under the petals or leaves. The pigments won't hammer through tape, so if you get little notches or squares in your images, check to make sure the tape is in the right place.

- Hammer gently. If you hammer too hard at first, the flower may squish out before you have a chance to get a good picture. Start slowly.

- If you're not happy with your image, try placing the leaf or petal with the other side down.

- If you don't get a sharp image, make sure you're hammering on a smooth surface. You can't hammer successfully on anything (such as a rock) that is not perfectly smooth.

- If you get little half-moons on your image, use a larger hammer.

- If the paper tears when you remove the tape, check to see that you're using removable tape.

- If the extra plant material doesn't come up with the tape, try scraping it off with the side of a knife. It will come off easier when it has dried completely.

Greeting Card *easy*

Instructions are given for these particular plants, but you can use other plants; if not, just tailor your message on the inside of the card to reflect the types of plants you use. (This project requires adult supervision.)

continued →

Greeting Card

You will need:

old sheet or towel

scraps of white construction paper (any size), for practice

practice plants (viola blossoms, leaves, and a fern)

smooth board

stack of old newspapers

paper towels

5-inch by 7-inch or 4-inch by 6-inch sheet of white construction paper

5 or 6 viola (or small pansy) blossoms

removable adhesive tape

scissors

hammer

4 or 5 pansy or viola leaves and a fern

several pieces of asparagus fern

iron

markers or colored pencils, if needed

9-inch by 12-inch colored construction paper (or other colored paper)

ruler

glue stick

narrow ribbon or trim (optional)

How to do it:

1 Cover your work area with a sheet or towel. Use your Art Skill (see page 106) to practice hammering flowers on a scrap of construction paper before you begin your project. Practice with the same kind of flowers and paper that you will use for your finished card.

2 Place a smooth board on top of the newspapers. Put a paper towel over this and the white construction paper on top of the paper towel.

3 Place one viola blossom facedown on the paper. Use removable tape to secure the petals. Make sure all the petals are taped down, then snip off the stem and other green parts. Hammer gently but thoroughly. Repeat with the other viola petals, stems, and leaves, creating a nice design.

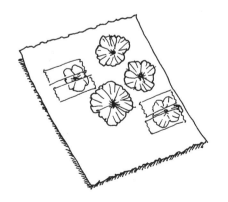

4 Cut pieces of the asparagus fern and hammer these onto your design. *Note:* If the fern won't hammer onto the paper, fill in the area by rubbing it directly onto the paper; this will transfer the color.

5 Leave the plants taped on, then use a warm (not hot) iron to press the paper on the *back* to heat-set the colors. Do not iron directly on the tape, as it will melt. Press for 20 seconds. Then remove the tape and any extra plant pieces. If you need to, fill in any blank spots with colored markers.

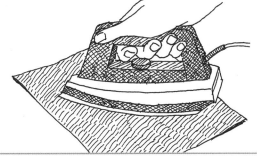

6 Fold the colored construction paper in half so it looks like a greeting card. Use the ruler to help center the hammered design on the front of the colored paper. Glue your design to the front of the card.

7 Cut narrow ribbon, if desired, or trim to fit around the edge of the white construction paper design. Glue it on. Write a greeting on the inside. Viola is the symbol for remembering friends, so send this card to friends you haven't seen for a while — and tell them that violas mean happy memories!

VARIATIONS

There are all sorts of cards you can make with hammered flowers and leaves. Make different sizes, or try some of the following:

- Hammer a design on white fabric. Use a glue stick to affix the decorated fabric to a piece of colored paper or fabric. Cut this to fit on a white card and glue it on.

- Make a collage on the front of a stiff white card by gluing on hammered images along with other natural treasures, such as pieces of bark, dried flowers, lichen, moss, and dried grass.

- Buy watercolor paper greeting cards. Hammer a design directly onto the front of the card. (Don't use slick paper; it won't take the hammering.)

- Hammer a design on a cone-shaped coffee filter. Cut out the design and glue it onto the front of a card.

- When you have a design you like a lot, take it to a photocopy store and have color copies made from it. This way, you can make lots of cards quickly.

Nature Journal *easy*

Hammering flowers and leaves is a great way to illustrate a nature journal, whether you design just the cover or do something on every page. First, though, decide what kind of journal you want to keep — see page 115 for ideas. (This project requires adult supervision.)

You will need:

old sheet or towel

smooth board

stack of old newspapers

paper towels

several pieces of white fabric, paper, or coffee filters

plants from the garden, woods, or fields

adhesive tape — removable for paper, regular for cloth

hammer

iron

plant identification guide (optional)

pen with ink that won't run or smear

scissors

4-inch by 6-inch photo album with solid-color cover (brown, green, or tan — something earthy-looking)

plain white paper, for writing on

craft glue

colored construction paper to cover the outside of album (optional)

JOURNAL IDEAS

There are many kinds of journals you can make. Here are some suggestions:

■ Write poems and use the hammered plants for illustrations.

■ Make a record of what grows in the woods and fields near your house, school, or camp, and use the hammered images for scientific illustrations (but remember, not all plants hammer well).

■ Write about what you see and like in nature.

How to do it:

1 Cover your work area with a sheet or towel. Use your Art Skill (see page 106) to practice hammering plants on a scrap of construction paper before you begin your project.

2 Place a smooth board on top of the newspapers. Put a paper towel over this and the fabric, paper, or coffee filter on top of the paper towel.

continued →

3 Place one plant facedown on the fabric. Use removable tape to secure it. Hammer gently but thoroughly.

4 Leave the plant taped on, then use a warm (not hot) iron to press the paper on the *back* to heat-set the colors. Do not iron directly on the tape, as it will melt. Press for 20 seconds.

5 Repeat steps 2 through 4 with each plant on a separate piece of fabric, paper, or coffee filter.

6 If you wish, use a plant identification guide to find out the name of the plant and write it on the same page as the hammered image.

7 Cut the fabric, paper, or coffee filters to fit and slip them into the plastic sleeves of the photo album.

8 Alternate a page of writing with a page of illustrations.

9 Choose a really nice hammered image for the front of the album. Cut it to fit, glue it to a piece of colored construction paper, then glue the whole thing onto the front of the album.

10 If you'd like, use a large sheet of colored paper to cover the back of the album as well.

Fantastic Creatures *easy*

An interesting thing you can do with hammered flowers is to make little figures. Go outside and look at the leaves and flowers you could use. A leaf with a long, narrow end makes a perfect beak. A rounded leaf makes a great body. Long, narrow petals make good feathers. You can cut plants into any shape you need, but the more natural shapes you use, the more charming your characters will be.

(This project requires adult supervision.)

You will need:

old sheet or towel

leaves and flowers

smooth board (such as a clip-board or a chopping board)

paper towels

white construction paper or small pieces of white fabric about 4 inches square

removable adhesive tape (avail-able at office or art supply stores) to use with paper or adhesive tape to use with fabric

hammer

iron

How to do it:

Cover your work area with a sheet or towel. Follow steps 1 through 6 of "Hammering on Paper" on page 107 or steps 1 through 3 of "Hammering on Cloth" on page 109.

Note: It's easier to keep everything in proportion if you start with the body, then add the head, legs, feet, tail, or whatever afterward. Let your imagination go wild — literally.

T-shirt challenging

Ferns are great for this project; the colors last longer than those of most other plants and don't wash out as easily. You'll have fun wearing this decorated T-shirt. The image is so beautiful — no one will believe you used only a hammer.

(This project requires adult supervision.)

You will need:

old sheet or towel

paper towels

smooth board

stack of old newspapers

white T-shirt, washed and dried thoroughly

adhesive tape

summer ferns

hammer

iron

clothes dryer

green fabric marker, if needed

½ cup salt

large flat pan

1 gallon water

spoon

To make this shirt completely washable and last for a long time, hammer your flowers (any kind) on a piece of fabric, then scan the image into the computer and print it out on T-shirt transfer paper (available at office supply stores). Follow the directions on the transfer paper to iron the design onto your T-shirt.

How to do it:

1 Cover your work area with a sheet or towel. Set a paper towel on top of the board and the board on top of the newspapers. Place the entire pile inside the T-shirt (this keeps the design from going through to the back).

2 Use adhesive tape to secure the ferns where you want them. Make sure they won't shift while you're hammering.

continued ⟶

3 Cover the ferns with a paper towel. Hammer carefully until all the ferns have been transferred. Make sure you've hammered thoroughly by looking carefully at the underside of the front of the T-shirt. If you need to, hammer some more.

4 When you have hammered all over the ferns, remove the paper towel. Leave the plant material taped on and carefully turn the T-shirt inside out.

5 With a warm (not hot) iron, heat-set the colors on the inside of the T-shirt for 20 to 30 seconds. Alternatively, remove the tape and put the T-shirt into the clothes dryer for 10 minutes.

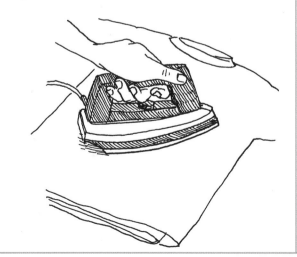

6 Turn the T-shirt right-side out. If you missed places, you can fill in the design with a green fabric marker.

7 Pour the salt into the pan. Add the water. Stir until the salt has dissolved. Place the prepared T-shirt in the salt solution for 3 minutes. Remove, wring out the excess water, and dry immediately in the clothes dryer. Do not dry it in the sun.

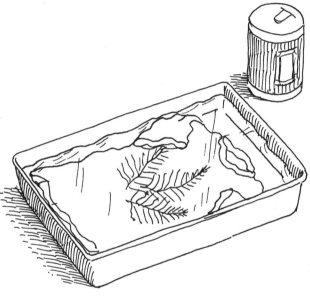

Note: You can wash the T-shirt by turning it inside out and rinsing with cold water on the gentle cycle. The dryer will not hurt the design, but try to keep it out of bright sunlight for too long. The colors will fade after a while.

Making Ink

People have been making and using ink ever since they have been making and using paper. The Chinese character for ink, *mo*, comes from two characters: *hei*, meaning black, and *t'u*, meaning earth. So ink, according to the Chinese, is black earth. In ancient times, ink was made from the soot from lamp smoke. Ink is a little different from paint in that it is usually a dark color and needs to have an even, smooth flow. (This project requires adult supervision.)

You will need:

piece of steel wool (not a soap pad)

glass jar with lid (such as a jelly jar)

½ cup white vinegar

½ cup water

small pot

2 tea bags

measuring spoons

plastic or glass cup

½ tablespoon white glue

plastic spoon

paintbrush or large feather

paper

iron (optional)

How to do it:

1 Place the steel wool in the jar and pour the vinegar over it. Put the lid on the jar. Allow it to sit in the sunshine (indoors or out) for at least 24 hours.

2 Boil the water in the pot, then add the tea bags. Remove from the heat and let steep for about 3 minutes. You should have a very dark, strong tea.

3 Measure 3 tablespoons of the steel wool–vinegar liquid into the cup. Add 3 tablespoons of the tea. Mix in the glue and stir well to combine.

4 Dip the paintbrush into the ink and write on the paper. This ink turns a darker color as it dries. For quick results, hold an iron a few inches above the paper on which you are writing, if desired.

Dyeing

Lots of familiar plants make great dyes, and you can find many of them in a flower or vegetable garden. Try bracken fern, carrot tops, chrysanthemums, coreopsis, dahlias, goldenrod, ivy, juniper berries, lichen, marigolds, onion skins, red cabbage, tansy, walnut shells, and zinnias (see pages 202–208 for descriptions of these and how to make dyes from each one).

Dyes show up best on white material. Be sure to wash any cloth before you dye it. Fabrics made from all-natural materials (cotton, silk, and linen, for example) dye best, but try other fabrics, too. The best wool for dyeing is a soft, thin wool called wool crepe. It's a little expensive, but you'll need only about ⅓ yard to do several of these projects. Cornhusks don't take the colors as quickly as do fabrics, but if you leave them in their dye baths long enough, they will eventually turn beautiful colors.

Dyeing materials always brings surprises. Different materials turn different colors. For example, wool usually turns a deeper color than cotton, even when they've been treated the same way. When you've experimented with different plants, make a dye chart. Cut small squares of different fabrics you have dyed and mark them with the name of the dye plant and the type of mordant used. Then you'll know how to get the colors you want.

Dyeing is accomplished in three stages.

step 1: Mordant the material.

step 2: Make a dye bath.

step 3: Dye the material.

Caution: The tools and materials you use for dyeing should *never* be used for cooking, even if they have been cleaned thoroughly. (This project requires adult supervision.)

Step 1: Mordant the material

To mordant means first to soak the material in a solution so that it will take the dye better. If you mordant, this must be the first step. It is optional, however. If you prefer, you can skip this step.

You will need:

rubber gloves

apron

4 tablespoons alum (you can sometimes get this in the canning department of a supermarket or in the silk-painting department of a craft store)

3 tablespoons cream of tartar (available in the spice section of a supermarket)

large stainless-steel or enamel pot (a small amount of material in a large pot take up the dyes more evenly than material crammed into a small pot)

5 quarts water

stovetop or electric burner

long-handled wooden or plastic spoon

½ yard washed white wool or cotton fabric, string, or yarn

bucket

How to do it:

1 Put on the rubber gloves and apron (and wear old clothes). Put the alum and the cream of tartar into the pot. Pour the water into the same pot.

2 Carefully put the pot onto the stove (don't slosh) and turn the heat on low. Stir for a few minutes, until the powders have dissolved.

3 Wet the fabric, string, or yarn in plain water and put it into the mordant (the alum and cream of tartar) solution. Poke it down with the spoon and try to get it as flat as possible. The material should be covered. If not, stir often to cover evenly. Simmer the solution for about 10 minutes.

4 Turn off the heat and let it cool, then lift out the fabric, string, or yarn, still wearing the rubber gloves. Put it into the bucket. Pour the alum solution either down the toilet or into a waste place outside.

5 Keep on the gloves and wring out the extra solution from your material and hang it up to dry on a shower curtain rod or outside until you are ready to use it.

Step 2: **Make a dye bath**

Create a dye bath by soaking plants in water, then heating the mixture in a pot until the water turns colors.

For making a dye bath with a specific plant, follow the instructions under that plant in the Nature Skills section (see pages 202–208). Always wear rubber gloves and an apron while dyeing.

You will need:

rubber gloves

apron

plant material for dyeing (see list on pages 202–208)

knife

large plastic tub or glass bowl

same pot used to mordant (see page 123)

stovetop or electric burner

strainer

large plastic tub or glass bowl

How to do it:

For roots, nuts, bark, leaves, and twigs:

1 Chop or tear up the material as much as possible. Place it in a large stainless-steel pot, and cover with water. Let it sit for a couple of days.

2 When the plant material is soft and releases color, place the pot on the stove. Turn the heat on low and simmer for a couple of hours.

3 Strain out the plant material over a large plastic tub or glass bowl.

Placing plant material in a large pot of water

For flowers:

1 Place a large quantity of blossoms (up to ½ potful) in a large stainless-steel pot.

2 Place the pot on the stove and turn the heat to low. Simmer for 20 minutes to several hours, until the blossoms yield no more color.

3 Strain out the plant material over a large plastic tub or glass bowl.

For onion skins and cabbage leaves:

1 Tear the skins or leaves into pieces, then soak them in water for 1 hour. Pour into a large stainless-steel pot.

2 Place the pot on the stove and turn the heat to high. Boil for ½ to 1¼ hours.

3 Strain out the plant material over a large plastic tub or glass bowl.

Simmering on the stove

Straining out plant material

TROUBLESHOOTING

If you're having trouble getting the colors or effect you want, try some of the following:

- If your material doesn't come out very dark, leave it in the dye bath longer, or try a different dye material.

- If your material looks splotchy and not evenly dyed, use less material and smooth it out in the pan more.

- If you want different colors using the same kind of dye, try mordanting on the cloth before you dye it.

Step 3: Dye the material

If you're going to mordant the fabric, do this before you put it into the dye bath. Soak the cloth or other material to be dyed in the dye bath until it changes color.

You will need:

apron or old clothes

rubber gloves

dye bath

same pot used to mordant and dye
(see page 123)

½ yard (or less) wet fabric or yarn

stovetop or electric burner

long-handled spoon

How to do it:

1 Put on the apron and rubber gloves. Prepare dye bath according to the instructions on pages 124–125. Pour it into the pot.

2 Put the fabric into the dye bath. Place the pot on the stove and turn the heat to low. Use the spoon to smooth out the material. The dye should cover the fabric.

3 Simmer for 10 minutes to 1 hour, depending on the kind of dye used (see pages 124–125 for dyeing times).

4 When the material has absorbed as much color as possible, turn off the heat and, with the material still in the bath, allow the solution to cool.

5 Remove the material, wring out the excess dye bath, and rinse it under cool water until no more color comes out. (Although this will lighten your dyed materials considerably, it is a necessary step.) Dry the material on a clothesline, but not in bright sunlight.

Purple Handbag challenging

You can use any dyed fabric to make this bag. If you don't like purple, try making a yellow bag dyed with marigold petals or a green one dyed with spinach leaves. Remember that wool turns a deeper color than cotton does. *Note:* If you really love these projects but don't want to go to the trouble of dyeing the fabric, just make them out of regular fabrics and decorate them any way you want. (This project requires adult supervision.)

continued →

Purple Handbag

You will need:

⅓ yard white or off-white wool crepe or ⅓ yard cotton fabric and 2 yards white cotton string or yarn

old sheet or towel

iron

pen

ruler

scissors

fabric glue, needle and thread, or sewing machine (get an adult to help you)

small clothespins

How to do it:

1 Wash the fabric and string, then dye them with purple cabbage leaves (see page 125 for how to make a dye with cabbage leaves and page 126 for how to dye material).

2 Cover your work area with a sheet or towel. Iron the dyed fabric to make it smooth. Using a pen and ruler, measure one piece of fabric 6 inches wide and 21 inches long. Measure another piece of fabric 3 inches wide and 36 inches long. Cut the pieces with scissors.

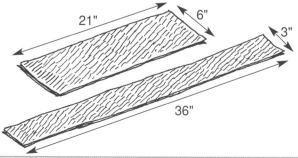

3 Fold the 21-inch piece of dyed fabric lengthwise 7 inches. This means 7 inches are doubled (to make a pocket) and 7 inches are a single layer of fabric to make the flap.

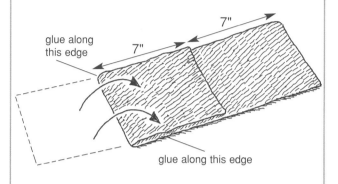

4 Either glue or stitch the sides of the doubled fold to make a pocket. Allow the glue to dry (this will take about 1 hour).

5 Take the longer piece of fabric and fold it in half lengthwise. This makes it 1½ inches wide. Press it with the iron.

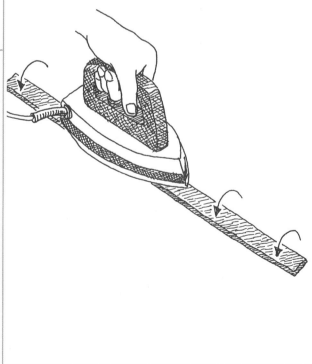

6 Fold it again lengthwise; this makes it about ¾ inches wide. Press it again. Glue together the long edges to make the strap. Use clothespins to hold it as it dries.

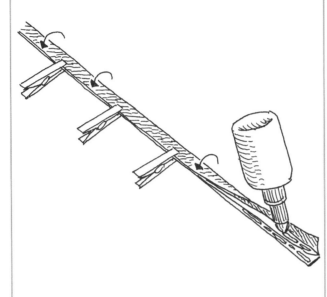

8 Glue the ends of the strap to the inside of the flap. If you want, fringe the edges of the bag by pulling threads up to the edge of the stitching or glue.

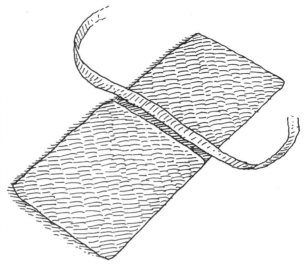

7 When the bag has dried, turn down the flap over the pocket. Decorate it by gluing or stitching on pieces of dyed string or yarn. Make spiral shapes or knots or just squiggles out of the string, then glue them onto the flap. Glue string to the strap as well, if desired.

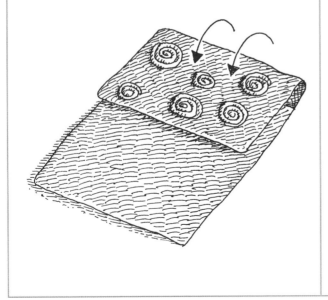

THE FIRST DYES

When people first began coloring cloth, they made dyes from the plants that grew around them. You could tell what kind of plants grew nearby by the color of their clothes. For example, the original plaid cloth from Scotland was colored soft gray, green, and blue, because lichens and moss were used as dyes. People who lived in hot, tropical regions wore brightly colored cloth, because brightly colored flowers grew in their area and they could make dyes from those. If you had to wear clothes dyed just with the plants that grow close to where you live, what color would they be?

Painting with Petals and Leaves

Plants will give up their colors when you simply rub them across a piece of paper. But this process is full of surprises. For example, bright pink vinca petals turn blue on paper. An orange marigold turns brown. Flowers that have petals all the same color give you clearer colors (for example, all yellow instead of yellow and orange mixed). Leaves with a shiny or leathery surface do not work as well as soft leaves. You'll also find that the kind of paper you use can make a difference. Because there is moisture in the petals, you will need to use a heavy paper to help keep your finished masterpiece from curling at the edges.

You will need:

old sheet or towel

different-colored petals and leaves

heavy watercolor or white construction paper

pen or marker

plant identification book, if needed

How to do it:

1 Cover your work area with a sheet or towel. Pick several petals of one flower. Roll them into a small ball or fold them into a rounded stick. Use your finger to push, pull, or rub them across the paper.

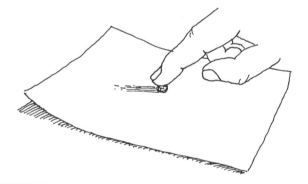

2 Experiment with different kinds of plants on different kinds of paper.

3 Make a chart showing each color and write the plant name next to it. Use a plant identification book if necessary.

Amulet Bag challenging

Many people like to take a special treasure with them wherever they go. It may be a stone, a feather, a piece of bark, herbs — whatever has special meaning for them. Ancient people called these *amulets*, charms, or tokens. Native Americans often carried their special treasures in a small leather pouch worn next to the skin. Although the bag described here is made out of dyed wool instead of leather, it looks almost the same. Fill your amulet bag with a pretty stone or something else small and precious.

(This project requires adult supervision.)

continued →

Amulet Bag

You will need:

⅛ yard white or off-white wool crepe and ½ yard white cotton string

old sheet or towel

iron

pen

ruler

scissors

fabric glue

BUTTERMILK PAINT

In Colonial times, beautiful, light-colored paints were made by mixing dyes and pigments with buttermilk. The problem with this was that it made the walls turn moldy! The solution? One old recipe book says: Add enough salt to the bucket of paint so that you can taste it. This will keep the mold down.

A spoonful of paint, anyone?

How to do it:

1 Wash the fabric and string, then dye them brown with tea or walnut shells (see page 208 for how to make a dye with walnut shells and page 126 for how to dye fabric).

2 Cover your work area with a sheet or towel. Iron the dyed fabric to make it smooth. Using the pen and ruler, measure a piece of dyed wool 3 inches wide by 10 inches long. Cut it out with scissors.

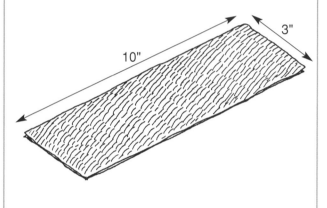

10"   3"

3 Fold up the bottom half 3 inches. Glue along the side edges to make the pocket.

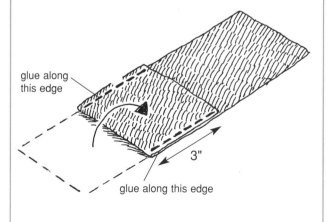

glue along this edge

3"

glue along this edge

4 Fold down the top half to make a heavy flap. Glue along the side edges.

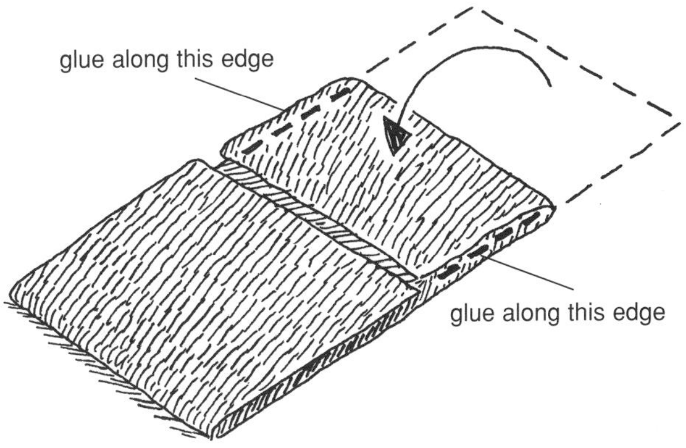

glue along this edge

glue along this edge

5 Cut another piece of wool 1 inch wide by 3 inches long. Use the scissors to make fringe along the long edge of this piece. Glue this piece to the bottom of the bag.

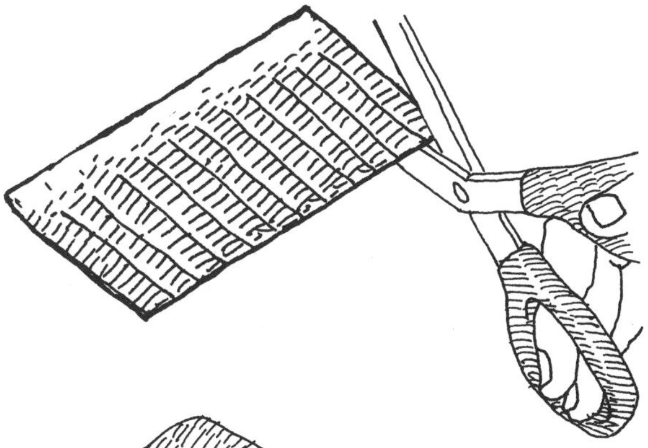

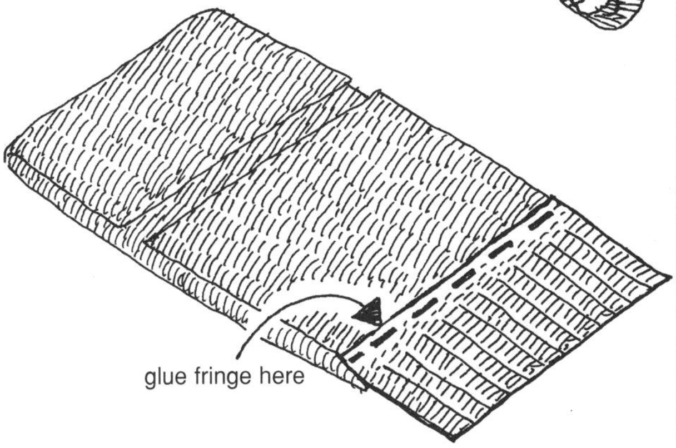

glue fringe here

6 For the strap, cut a piece of dyed string 30 to 36 inches long. Make sure it is long enough to fit over your head easily when attached to the bag. Glue the ends of the string to the inside of the bag where the flap folds over.

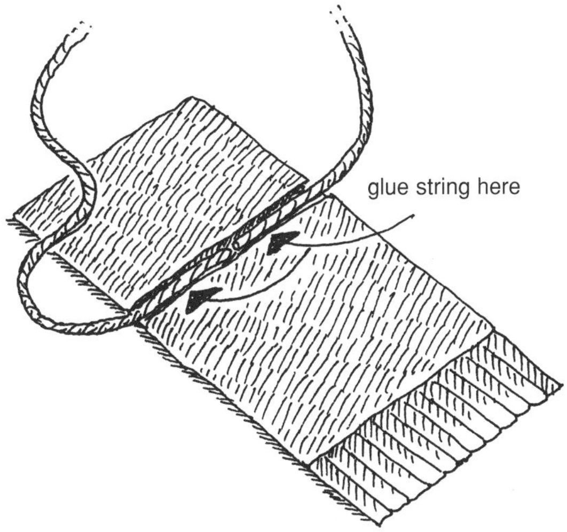

glue string here

7 Cut two more pieces of string about 4 inches long. Tie knots in the ends of each piece. Glue one knot to the bottom of the flap and the other to the front of the bag. Let dry. Tie the strings together to keep the bag closed.

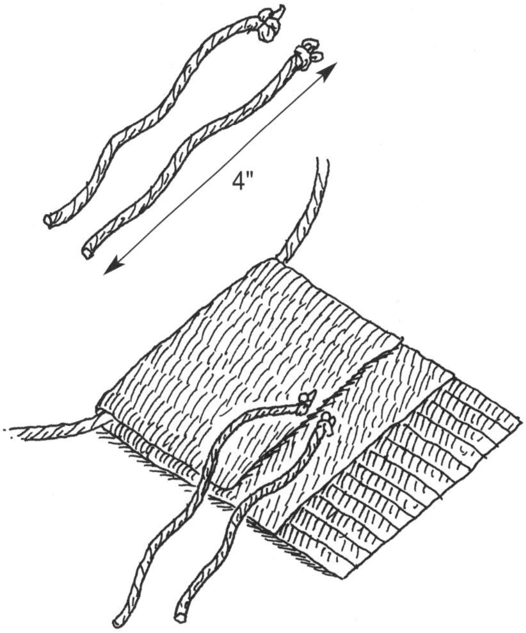

4"

Sachets medium

You can make pretty little bags from dyed fabric and fill them with flower potpourri. Place these bags in a chest of drawers to make your clothes smell good, attach them to the top of a gift box, or give them away as presents. Everyone loves these lovely, fragrant bags. (Dyeing fabric requires adult supervision.)

You will need:

8-inch by 6-inch piece of white or off-white wool crepe or cotton and 12 inches of white cotton string

old sheet or towel

fabric glue

¼ cup potpourri

How to do it:

1 Wash the fabric and string, then dye them yellow with marigolds (see page 206 for how to make a dye from marigolds and page 126 for how to dye fabric).

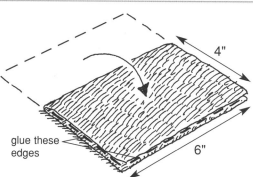

glue these edges

4"

6"

2 Cover your work area with a sheet or towel. Fold the dyed fabric in half, to make a piece that measures 4 inches by 6 inches. Glue along the bottom and side. Let dry.

3 When completely dry, gently turn the bag inside out. Reglue where necessary.

4 Place the potpourri in the bag. Tie it closed with string.

African Design medium

Many African designs are geometric and made from brown and black dyes. Although it's hard to make a black dye, brown is pretty simple to create. To make it a little easier, use a combination of brown-dyed cloth glued to black paper. Although the directions here are for doing this on paper (which can be slipped into the front of a binder or framed for a great piece of art), you can do the same thing on a piece of black fabric or even a T-shirt. (This project requires adult supervision.)

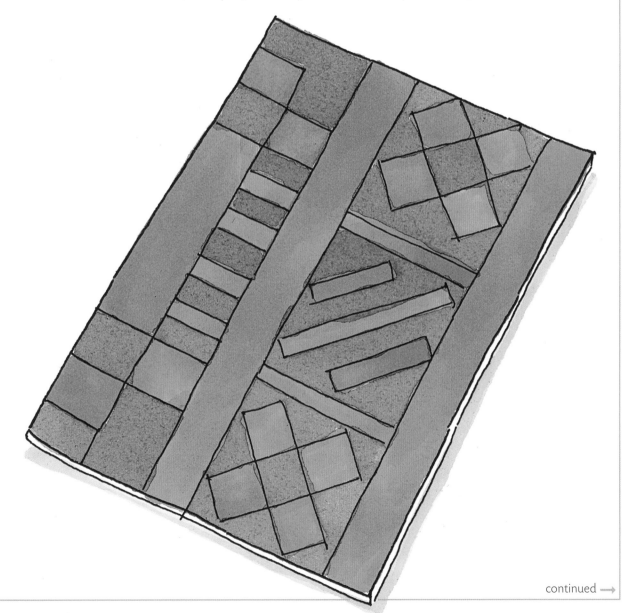

continued ⟶

African Design

You will need:

¼ yard white or off-white wool crepe or cotton

old sheet or towel

iron

ruler 1 inch wide, 12 inches long

pen

scissors

sheet of heavy black paper 8½ inches by 11 inches or larger

craft glue or fabric glue stick

How to do it:

1 Wash the fabric, then dye it brown with walnut shells (see page 208 for how to make a dye from walnut shells and page 126 for how to dye fabric).

2 Cover your work area with a sheet or towel. Lay out the dyed fabric on a flat surface. Iron it to make it smooth.

3 Place the edge of the ruler along the long edge of the fabric. Use a pen to carefully mark the outline of the ruler on the fabric. Carefully cut out this piece. It should be 1 inch wide by 12 inches long.

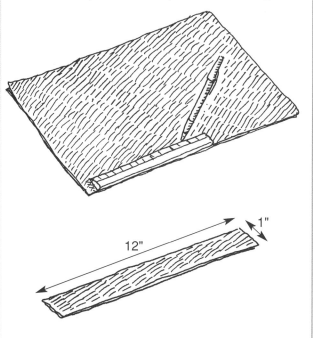

4 Place the fabric back on the flat surface and put the ruler along the cut edge. Cut this out (you should now have two pieces of the same size).

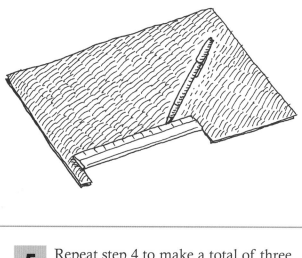

5 Repeat step 4 to make a total of three pieces of fabric.

6 Cut out different shapes from two of the long strips. For squares, fold up one end of the long strip to form a triangle and cut along this edge. When you unfold it, it's a square. When you turn it to the side, it's a diamond. If you cut it in half, it's a triangle.

7 Fold the third strip lengthwise and press with an iron along the fold. Use this as a cutting line. You should have two pieces that are 12 inches by ½ inch.

cut along fold

8 Arrange the various fabric pieces on the black paper. Make up your own design or get ideas from greeting cards, wrapping paper, or fabrics showing African designs. When you have a design you like, glue the pieces onto the paper.

Use different colors of dyed fabrics to make a "quilt." Follow the directions for the African Design project, but put them into a quilt design instead of an African design. If you need some ideas about quilt designs, there are lots and lots of books about quilts.

Making Paint

Most basic paint recipes call for three important ingredients: color (usually from rocks or plants), something to make it flow easily off the paintbrush, and something that makes it stick to the surface being painted.

When you begin mixing plant pigments (colors), you'll soon discover that they're quick to change their color when mixed with other substances. This is because they undergo a chemical change. For example, adding something very acidic, such as vinegar or lemon juice, to ground-up violets makes the purple liquid turn reddish. If you add something that has no acid in it, such as baking soda, it turns green. This allows you to change the color of many natural paints. Besides, it's fun to feel like a mad scientist. If you really want to be scientific about it, take notes and make a chart that shows the different colors and how you made them.

You will need:

old sheet or towel

mortar and pestle or a small bowl and spoon

pigments from the following list (whatever you have available):

◎ 5–10 brightly colored flowers

◎ a few rocks and lumps of soil: red clay, chalk, yellow and red ocher, or colored rocks

◎ ½ cup potting soil, other colors of natural soil

◎ small piece of charcoal or burned wood

several small bowls

1 egg

fork

spoon

paintbrush

scrap paper

2 tablespoons lemon juice

2 tablespoons baking soda

How to do it:

1 Cover your work area with a sheet or towel. Use the mortar and pestle to grind up each pigment as fine as you can. No matter what you are using, keep grinding until there are no separate pieces left, or as close to that as possible. Put each pigment into its own bowl.

2 Break the egg and separate the white from the yolk. Place them in separate bowls. Use the fork to beat the egg white a little so that it will pour more easily.

3 Add a drop or two of egg white to each of the ground pigments. Add egg white a drop at a time until the "paint" is thin enough to flow off the paintbrush onto a piece of scrap paper.

4 Change the color of your paint by adding lemon juice one drop at a time. Change it again by adding baking soda one sprinkle at a time.

5 Add a few drops of the egg yolk to some of the ground pigments and see whether you get different results.

COLOR EXAMPLES

- **Reddish brown from red clay (or potter's clay)**
- **Dark brown from potting soil**
- **Black from charcoal or burned wood**
- **Blue-green from blue lobelia blossoms**
- **Purple from pink dianthus petals**
- **Pink from pink dianthus petals and lemon juice**
- **Yellow-green from pink dianthus petals and baking soda**
- **Yellow from yellow marigold petals**

Body Paint *easy*

Throughout the ages, people have worn paint on their bodies as well as on their clothes. There are many reasons for this. Some ancient peoples, who lived in very cold climates, put paint mixed with oil or grease onto their bodies to help protect them from the weather. People also have worn body paint as an artistic expression. Some Native American tribes wore paint on their faces, chests, arms, and legs before they went into battle. They did this, in part, to intimidate their enemies, but more often they painted symbols on their bodies because they believed it would protect them from harm.

You will need:

paint (*see pages 138–139*)

small paintbrush

How to do it:

Follow the directions on pages 138–139 for making paint. Don't get any of these substances in your eyes, and don't leave any of them on your skin too long. Have fun, be artistic, and make your body a masterpiece!

BEAUTIFUL BUT SAFE

When you make your own body paint, make *sure* you use materials that won't irritate or harm your skin. You can test for this by placing a tiny dab of the paint on your arm and leaving it for an hour or so to see whether it irritates your skin. Most rocks and clays are fine, as are wood ashes and charcoal. Be careful if you use the juice from berries, though, because many berries are poisonous. The edible ones — blackberry, mulberry, and elderberry — are probably the safest to use.

Painted Quiver challenging

This project combines several Art Skills, including dyeing and painting, and the results are great. You can use this same idea to cover a book or make a bag. You can make many different kinds of designs on the fabric and use many different colors, but simple, geometric shapes are easy and effective. (Dyeing fabric requires adult supervision.)

continued →

Painted Quiver

You will need:

old sheet or towel

cardboard mailing tube 3 inches in diameter and 18 to 20 inches long

2 pieces of dyed wool: one about 13 inches wide and at least 1 inch longer than the tube and the other 3 inches by 14 inches

fabric glue

scissors

clothespins

ruler

2 leather laces, each 40 inches long

red clay paint (see pages 138–139) or charcoal, charred stick, or charcoal pencil

charcoal spray protector, if using charcoal

How to do it:

1 Cover your work area with a sheet or towel. Place the cardboard tube lengthwise on top of the longer piece of dyed wool. Position it so that the bottom of the tube is even with the bottom of the wool.

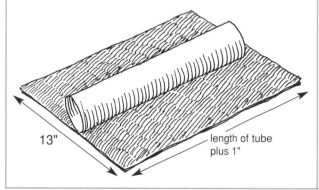

13"

length of tube plus 1"

2 "Draw" a strip of glue from the bottom of the tube to the top in one straight line. Press one edge of the wool onto the glue and allow it to dry.

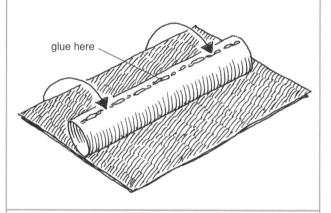

glue here

3 Put another strip of glue around the bottom and top edges of the tube and along the remaining long edge of the wool. Wrap the wool around the tube, pressing into the glue, covering the entire tube. Allow it to dry.

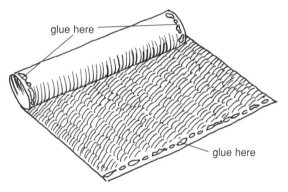

glue here

glue here

4 Cut the top of the wool even with the top of the tube.

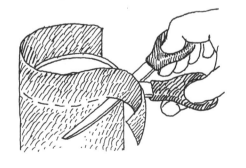

5 Fold the smaller piece of wool in half, making it 1½ inches wide and 14 inches long. Glue together the edges. Use clothespins to help keep the edges closed until the glue dries thoroughly.

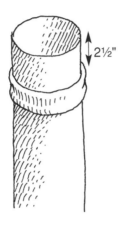

14"

1½"

6 Wrap the small piece of wool around the covered tube, overlapping the ends and leaving a 2½-inch margin at the top (use the ruler to measure). Glue in place to make a cuff. Allow the glue to dry thoroughly.

2½"

7 Wrap one of the leather laces around the cuff and tie it at the back, leaving a tail. Cut the tail of the lace and save it. Let dry.

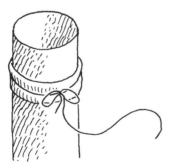

8 Slip one end of the short piece of lace between the tube and the cuff at the back. Pull the lace through and tie the ends, making a long loop.

9 Slip the remaining leather lace between the tube and the cuff at the back as well. Make as small a loop as possible, leaving one end long.

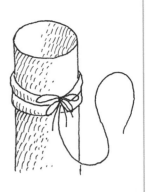

10 To decorate the quiver, turn it so that the back of the cuff is on a flat surface and the front of the quiver is facing you. Decorate it with the design of your choice, using red clay paint or charcoal. If you use charcoal, when you have completed your design, spray it with charcoal spray protector so the charcoal will not smear.

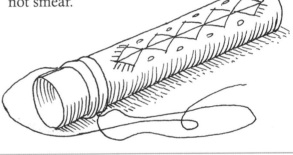

11 To wear, place the quiver on your back. Bring the leather loop over your right shoulder. Bring the single lace underneath your left arm. Slip the long, single lace through the loop at the front of your body and tie wherever is most comfortable.

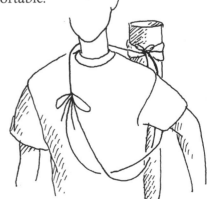

Part Six

Flowers and Leaves

Soon after people figured out how to make the items they needed for everyday life, they figured out how to make them more beautiful. They did this by using nature for decoration. If you look around with fresh eyes, you'll begin to see beauty that you never noticed before. Look at the light green lichen on a tree trunk and you'll soon realize how frilly and intricate it is. Notice the fungus on a log and suddenly you'll be seeing bands of color as pretty as a rainbow. Shells, with their intricate shapes and patterns, are really interesting if you take the time to look at them.

Making Flowers Last

One challenge you'll face in using flowers for decorations is how to make them last. You can always put fresh flowers in a glass of water and they'll be pretty for a few days, but what if you want to preserve them? Fortunately, there are ways to make flowers keep their shape and color even when they are not in water. Drying and pressing are the two most common methods, and both offer flowers that are excellent for use in many crafts.

HEALING WITH HERBS

In Europe during the Middle Ages (A.D. 500–1500), it was up to the mother to heal her family, and she would often grow herbs and flowers for that purpose. Many women even had a special room in the house — called the stillroom — in which they dried plants and made the concoctions they used for remedies.

Although dried-flower crafts are popular today, people have been drying flowers for centuries. For example, the ancient Egyptians used dried flowers and herbs to make their houses smell good and to heal them when they were sick. Because many valuable chemicals are found in flowers and herbs, the ancient Greeks and Romans used dried plants for medicines.

Pressing Flowers

Eventually, though, people noticed that the flowers they were grinding up to make potions were also beautiful to look at. By the 1800s, when Queen Victoria came to the throne in England, dried-flower decorations had become very popular. It was during Victorian times, too, that people began to place flowers between the pages of a book and discovered that as the paper absorbed the excess moisture from the blossoms, the flowers sometimes kept their shape and remained colorful. Pressed flowers, then, became a way to "paint" a floral picture without picking up a paintbrush, and anyone could create attractive pictures using real flowers and leaves.

As with all nature art, however, people had to use whatever they could find — or buy or trade for. In the same way, you'll use things that you can find. The trick is not in finding beautiful objects every day but in finding beauty in everyday objects.

Drying Flowers

The basic idea of drying flowers is to, well, dry them so they keep their shape and color for a long time. No matter how well you dry flowers, though, they will fade after a while. It may take years, but eventually they'll begin to lose their bright colors. Not to worry — even faded flowers are beautiful.

If you don't have a garden or if you don't have a place to dry flowers, you can always buy dried flowers at a craft store or a supermarket.

The easiest and quickest way to dry flowers is simply to hang them upside down for a few weeks. This method works well for the following flowers: black-eyed Susan, cockscomb, dahlia, globe amaranth, goldenrod, larkspur, lavender, rose, statice, strawflower, and yarrow. Some flowers dry better when you stand them upright rather than hanging them upside down. These include baby's breath, hydrangea, and various grasses.

SAY IT WITH FLOWERS

What in the world is a tussie mussie? During Victorian times, little bouquets were tied with lace and ribbon and given to friends. These were called tussie mussies. Each flower had a special meaning. For example, yellow coreopsis meant "always cheerful," carnation meant "admiration," phlox meant "hope for sweet dreams." Send your own flower message by surrounding a dried-flower bouquet with a piece of lace or a paper doily and tying it with a piece of ribbon.

You will need:

fresh flowers

paper towels

twistie ties, string, or raffia

How to do it:

1 If you are picking flowers from a garden, pick them in the morning after the dew has dried. Try to pick on a dry day — not after it has been raining. Pick flowers with long stems. Choose flowers that have just opened fully. If they are already dropping petals, they will not dry well. If you need to, use a paper towel to dry off any wet places.

2 Gather the flowers into a small bundle (three or four stalks of black-eyed Susan, for example) or dry a single flower (such as a rose).

3 Turn the flowers upside down and spread out the flower heads so that they barely touch. Secure the stems with a twistie tie (one of those little covered wire things that come with plastic bags).

4 Hang the bundles upside down on a nail or a hook in a cool, dry place. An attic is good; usually a basement is too damp for proper air-drying. An extra closet in the house is also a good place to dry flowers. Do not place the stems in direct sunlight; this will cause the colors to fade quickly.

5 For flowers that dry better standing upright, such as baby's breath and statice, place them in a vase, without water, and allow them to dry.

Dried-Flower Bouquet *easy*

These are simple to create and make great little gifts for any mom, grandmother, teacher, or anyone else. How do you use a bouquet? Tie a long ribbon and hang it on a drawer knob. Or put a short ribbon on it and tie it on a gift box. Or put a pin on the back and use it as a corsage.

You will need:

old sheet or towel

small bundle of dried flowers, all the same kind or different kinds

spray of dried baby's breath

thin wire or a twistie tie

ribbon in a matching or contrasting color

How to do it:

1 Cover your work area with a sheet or towel. The bouquet will have a front and a back. Place the prettiest parts of the dried-flower stalks so they all face outward. Put more uneven parts toward the back. If you have a single, special flower, such as a rose, insert this into the center and allow the other flowers to fan out around it.

2 Place the pieces of baby's breath among the other flowers to fill in any bare spots. Tie the stems together with the wire or twistie.

3 Tie the ribbon around the stems to hide the wire. Make a bow. Add more ribbon for hanging, if desired.

Dried-Flower Garden *easy*

You can make an amazing little garden — on paper! Although I've included suggestions for a formal design, you can actually design this any way you want. Look at some gardens and study how they are laid out, or look in books or magazines. Some gardens are very formal, with straight lines and flowers planted in shaped beds; others are much more natural-looking, with curves and wooded paths. Use your imagination and create a garden that pleases you. If you love doing this, you just might have a future in garden design!

continued →

Dried-Flower Garden

You will need:

old sheet or towel

several slender, straight sticks or the straight stems of lavender

heavy paper or poster board, about 9 inches by 12 inches (or any size you want)

hot glue gun and glue sticks or craft glue (see Glue Gun Caution! on page 7)

green sheet moss

dried flowers (for example, larkspur, lavender, roses, statice) and leaves

small ornament

sand, pebbles, pieces of bark (optional)

hook

Dried flowers make easy and quick decorations for all kinds of things. Take a plain wooden box or bag (available at a craft store) and glue dried flowers to the outside to make a gift or decoration.

How to do it:

1 Cover your work area with a sheet or towel. Arrange the sticks on the paper so they create four planting beds — one in each corner — and make four paths that meet in the center. Break the sticks to size, if necessary. Glue down each of the sticks.

2 Apply glue atop the sticks, then glue tiny pieces of moss on top of the sticks. If you use a hot glue gun, push the moss onto the glue with an extra stick instead of using your fingers. If you use craft glue, be patient; it takes a little longer for the glue to dry, but it does work. Should the moss start sticking to you, stop and wash the glue off your hands. Keep gluing moss onto the sticks until you have covered them, creating little green hedges around the paths.

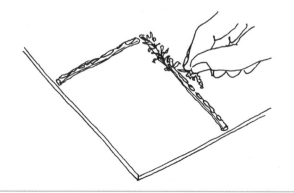

3 Place dried flowers and leaves in each of the four corner beds. You can fill the beds with flower heads or leave the stems on the blossoms and "plant" them in rows. Glue in place.

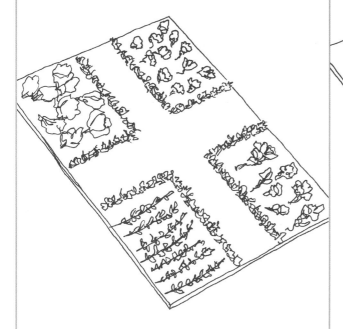

4 Place an ornament or some other eye-catching item in the center of the garden. You can use something as simple as a tiny vine wreath or as complicated as another flower bed. Glue in place.

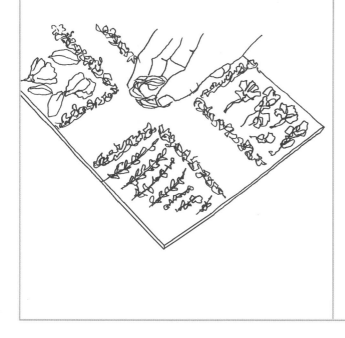

5 If desired, glue sand, pebbles, or pieces of bark to the paths. Glue a hook onto the back for hanging.

This particular design is supposed to hang on the wall, but you could also make a tabletop garden. This way, you can stand things up in it. Add a twig fence, an arbor or a gate, or a tiny birdbath made out of clay. Don't forget to make a bird, too! This would be lovely as the front garden for a dollhouse or as a scene for a model railroad.

Make one of the elf houses (see pages 44–53) and create an entire woodland scene around it. Make trees out of twigs placed in clay bases (see page 29) and make mushrooms from small pieces of clay.

Dried-Flower Fairy

challenging

This project is for a beautiful little fairy in shades of white and light brown. You could make several and hang them on the Christmas tree (she looks like an angel) or in a window.

You will need:

old sheet or towel

scissors

12–16 long strands of raffia

ruler or measuring tape

craft glue or hot glue gun and glue sticks (see Glue Gun Caution! on page 7)

scissors

poppy seed head, dried

dried grass (try to find some with a natural curve to it)

small bundle of dried flowers

FLOWER POWER

Even though you have probably always noticed flowers, you'll begin to appreciate them in new ways as you look for just the right blooms to complete your projects. The shape, color, and size of leaves and blossoms will mean something different to you when you need them for a project.

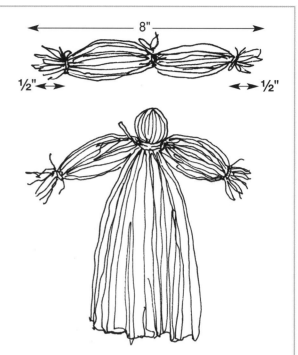

How to do it:

1 Cover your work area with a sheet or towel. Cut six to eight strands of raffia 10 to 12 inches long. Gather the strands and make sure they are neat and not tangled. Cut a smaller piece of raffia and use it to tie the strands together in the center.

2 Fold over the raffia bundle in the center (where it's tied) and use another short piece of raffia to tie the bundle about ½ inch from the folded top. This forms the body and the neck.

3 Cut six to eight pieces of raffia about 8 inches long. Tie them together at the center to form arms and again about ½ inch from each end to form hands. Glue the center of the arms to the back of the body.

4 Clip off the stem of the poppy seed head, leaving only about 1 inch. Glue the seed head to the neck of the raffia body to make the head.

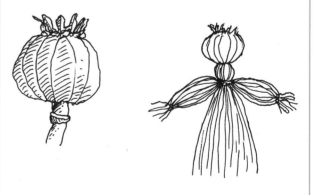

5 Glue several strands of dried grass to the back for wings. Glue the hands together and place a small bundle of dried flowers in her arms.

Magic Wand *easy*

What good is a fairy godmother without her magic wand? Or, for that matter, what good is a magician without a wand? Make the wand of your dreams by gluing together sticks, moss, and flowers. Although directions are given here for a wand covered with flowers, instead of blossoms you could glue moss or lichen onto the stick and small pinecones onto the ends.

old sheet or towel

craft glue or hot glue gun and glue sticks (see Glue Gun Caution! on page 7)

3 straight sticks, each 4 to 5 inches long

long straight stick (not too heavy) cut so that it is the right size for a good wand

sheet moss

dried flowers

How to do it:

1 Cover your work area with a sheet or towel. Glue the three short sticks together to form a star. When that has dried, glue the center of the star to one end of the long stick.

2 Glue small pieces of moss and dried flowers to the star-shaped sticks. If you want, glue a different-color flower to each end and the center of the star.

Flower Headband medium

Whether you want to play dress-up or need to dress up for real, this dried-flower headpiece is stunning! It's best to start with a store-bought headband. Don't get one that is stretchy. A hard one that fits on just the top of your head will be easier to work with. A bridal headband is best. If you go to a shop that sells bridal fabrics, you can find a headband made with fake pearls. That headband would make a charming base for your flowers.

continued →

Flower Headband

You will need:

old sheet or towel

scissors

5 small dried roses

headband

measuring tape, if needed

craft glue or hot glue gun and glue sticks (see Glue Gun Caution! on page 7)

clothespin, if needed

1 pink larkspur

1 blue lavender

How to do it:

1 Cover your work area with a sheet or towel. Leaving about ½ inch, clip the stem off one rose. You want all the sepals (the green parts underneath the blossom) to be attached to the remaining stem.

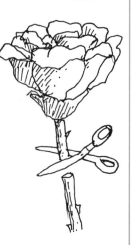

2 Find the center of the headband (use a measuring tape, if necessary) and glue one rose to it. Because a rose has layers and layers of petals, you'll need to put several dots of glue onto the petal layers so that the rose won't fall off the outer petal that's glued to the headband.

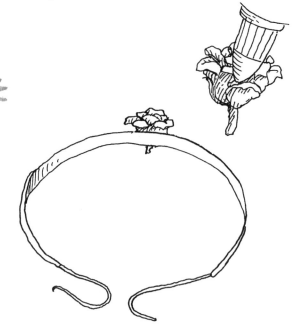

Note: If you're working with craft glue, use a clothespin to keep the rose attached to the headband until the glue dries.

You can make a necklace in a similar way. The base will have to be something wide enough for the flowers to stick to. Try a piece of satin ribbon. Measure the length of the ribbon so it will go over your head easily, then tie it in back. Place small dried flowers on the ribbon and glue them in place until you have covered it entirely (or at least the part in front).

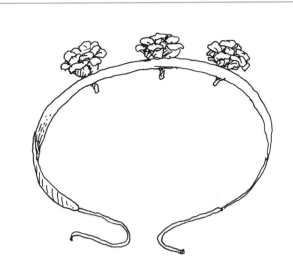

3 Leave a space (about 1 inch) and affix another rose to the headband in the same way, gluing the petal layers together. Move 1 inch to the other side of the center rose and glue on another rose in the same manner.

4 Skip another inch or so and glue a fourth rose onto the headband, almost at the end. Glue the fifth rose on the other side, almost at that end.

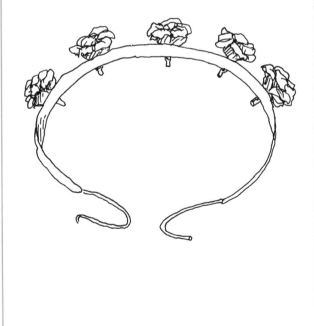

5 Fill in the spaces between the roses by gluing on bits and pieces of lark-spur and lavender. Let the headband dry completely before you try to put it on.

To make a fresh-flower necklace, take a piece of clear fishing line and thread it through a needle. Make sure the fishing line is long enough to make a circle that will easily go over your head. Make a knot at one end, then thread small flowers onto the line. In spring you can use dianthus, honeysuckle, jasmine, larkspur, phlox, and violas. In summer, try black-eyed Susans, cosmos, daisies, marigolds, small roses and rosebuds, and small zinnias.

Pressing Plants

You'll have a great time pressing flowers and leaves. Pressed plants are wonderful for illustrating and decorating almost anything. The basic idea is to put plant material into a book or special press to flatten it and absorb moisture without losing the color and shape. Certain plants, of course, press better than others. Some plants look as though they would be fine to press, but then they lose their color too quickly. Anything that has a large flowering head (such as a carnation) is difficult to press, because there are just too many layers for it to flatten out and dry well.

The best plants for pressing are those that have thin petals and leaves and an interesting shape. Look for things such as curly tendrils on grapevines and petals that have lots of veins or detailed patterns. Asters, cosmos, curly vines, ferns, grass, honeysuckle, hydrangea, larkspur, lobelia, pansies, pelargonium (geranium), primrose, and flat roses are all great. See Nature Skills (pages 203–208) to learn how to identify these plants. In addition to the projects in this section, see pages 106–109 on hammering flowers for more ideas. Most of the projects that use hammered flowers can be done with pressed flowers as well.

You will get the very best results if you use a plant press, which is made up of two boards, held together with screws at each corner, and a stack of blotting paper.

You will need:

plants for pressing

blotting paper

scissors

heavy books or plant press

bricks, if needed

How to do it:

1 Place the plants on the blotting paper, positioning them so that they are not touching one another. Remember that when the plants are pressed, they will retain their shape exactly as you placed them. Make sure you position the plants as you want them. Unless it is a small, thin stem and flower, it's best to snip off the stem and press it separately. For a flower that has a hard center, such as black-eyed Susan, push on the center to flatten it with your fingers as much as possible. Cover with another piece of blotting paper.

2 Place the blotting paper between the pages of a heavy book, then put something heavy, such as other books or bricks, on top of your book press to weight it down. It may take a little longer for the plants to dry completely, and the colors may not stay quite as vibrant, but pressing in a book is very fast and very easy.

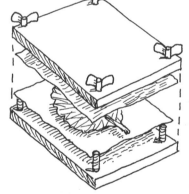

3 If you enjoy this craft, you may want to buy a plant press. Place the blotting paper between the boards of the plant press and screw down each corner as tightly as you can.

TWO IN ONE

Although some flowers are nearly impossible to press as they are, you can take them apart — even carnations — and press the parts separately. Daffodils, too, seem too difficult, but split the blossom in half and press each one and you'll have two for the price of one! Cover each one with another piece of blotting paper.

Name Mug *easy*

You can find at craft stores clear plastic mugs that snap apart to allow you to place a design inside. And what better design than your name (or Mom or Dad), written in pressed leaves and flowers? Make each letter out of pressed plants, then put together in just the right way.

You will need:

old sheet or towel

plastic mug

white paper, if needed

pencil

scissors

pressed flowers and leaves

craft glue

How to do it:

1 Cover your work area with a sheet or towel. Take apart the mug and remove the inside sheet. If the sheet is plain white, you can just use this. (This may have a design for coloring on it; just ignore it.)

2 If the inside sheet is not white, place it on top of a piece of white paper, trace the outline with a pencil, and cut out the white paper so it is exactly the size of the inside sheet.

3 Place the paper back inside the plastic holder and note where the paper overlaps. Remove the paper and use the pencil to mark where the paper overlaps so you don't put any design onto a place that will later be covered up.

4 Lay the paper flat. Spell out your name (or Mom or Dad or Grandma or whatever name you want) using flowers and leaves to "write" with. You may have to trim some of the plants with scissors. Leave space at each end of the paper, so the letters don't run into each other when you wrap it around the mug. Glue the plants to the paper. Allow the glue to dry.

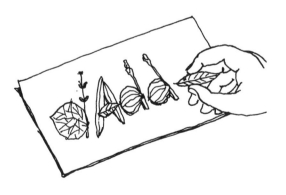

5 Place the paper back inside the holder. Put the mug back together. *Note:* Don't put your mug into the dishwasher; wash it by hand, very carefully.

Fern Print medium

Spend some time finding a wide variety of ferns; it will make the finished product even better. If you can find them, pick some spore stalks (stems with brown things on them) as well. You need to do the project in two steps. First, pick and press the ferns. Allow them to dry for 7 to 10 days. Then assemble the picture. Your print will be elegant enough to hang in a museum!

You will need:

variety of ferns

heavy book and blotting paper or plant press

old sheet or towel

heavy paper (such as watercolor paper) the same size as or bigger than the frame

picture frame 12 inches by 16 inches

pencil

scissors

craft glue

How to do it:

1 Press the ferns carefully (follow the directions on page 161), making sure they have nice curves and lines. If you can find the same fern in different stages, press all of them. For example, a young, curved fern looks very different from a mature, fat one. Allow the ferns to dry for 7 to 10 days.

2 Cover your work area with a sheet or towel. If the paper is larger than the frame, take out the back piece of the frame, lay it on the paper, and trace the outline with a pencil. Cut the paper on the pencil line so it is the same size as the frame.

3 Set the ferns in a pleasing design on the paper. If you want, write the name of each fern underneath it. Glue each fern to the paper. Make sure that each one is secure. Put the fern design into the frame.

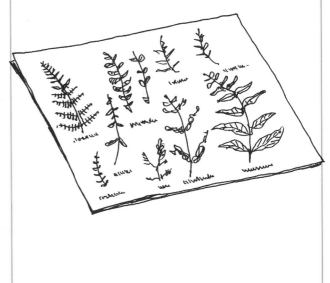

Window or Tree Ornaments medium

Almost any craft store carries small plastic Christmas tree ornaments designed for use with cross-stitch projects. Instead of needlework, place pressed flowers and leaves inside the ornament. This project is simple — go ahead, make a bunch of ornaments during the holidays and give them away as gifts.

old sheet or towel

plastic ornaments

white paper, pencil, and scissors, if needed

pressed flowers or leaves

craft glue

wide clear packaging tape (such as wide Scotch Tape)

How to do it:

1 Cover your work area with a sheet or towel. Pop out the back of an ornament.

2 If the back is white, use this as a base. If it is gray or colored or unattractive, place the back on a piece of white paper, trace the outline with a pencil, and cut out a piece of paper exactly the size of the back.

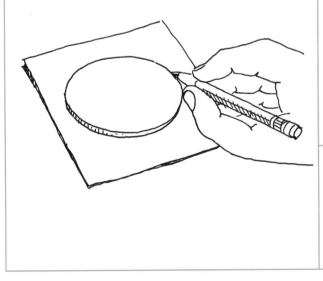

3 Place pressed flowers or leaves on the ornament back in a pleasing pattern. Single leaves or blossoms often make the best designs. Use red blossoms or green leaves for Christmas. Use dots of glue to secure the plants to the back.

4 Cut a piece of tape a little larger than the back. Gently place it over the plant design. Be careful that the plants don't jump off the paper and onto the tape before you're ready. To guard against this, hold the tape flat, just above the ornament, and lower it quickly and evenly. If you get a plant that just won't cooperate, start again and use more glue before you put on the clear tape. Trim the tape close to the edge of the ornament.

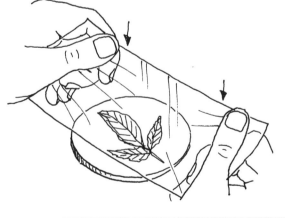

5 Pop the back of the ornament into the front piece and hang it up.

Funny Faces medium

What makes up a face? Eyes, nose, and mouth (and a few other things!). It's fun to make faces with leaves and petals — and even more fun to mix them up. To make really funny and unusual faces, take time to choose and press leaves and flowers that look like the facial features you'll need.

You will need:

old sheet or towel

pressed flowers, including several circular ones

pressed leaves and ferns

unlined 3 by 5 index cards

craft glue

clear packaging tape

hole punch

three-ring binder 9 inches by 12 inches

How to do it:

1 Cover your work area with a sheet or towel. Select pressed flowers and leaves that look like eyes and eyebrows. Place them on the index card and try a variety of expressions. When you like the look of the design, place a dot of glue on each plant and secure it to the card.

2 Gently place the tape over the plant design. Be careful the plants don't "jump" off the card and onto the tape before you're ready. To guard against this, hold the tape flat, just above the card, and lower it quickly and evenly.

3 Take another index card for the nose. A single leaf or part of a leaf makes a fine nose. Glue it on the card and repeat step 2 to cover it with tape.

4 Now the mouth. On another index card, lay several petals end to end to make a smile or cut a piece of fern to make a smile (or a frown) with teeth.

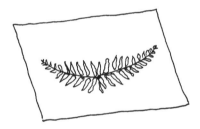

5 Repeat steps 1 through 4 two times so that you have three eye cards, three nose cards, and three mouth cards. Make each one different.

6 Punch a hole in the left edge of each card and put the cards into the binder, with the eye cards in the top ring, the nose cards in the middle ring, and the mouth cards in the bottom ring. Flip and turn the cards to make funny faces.

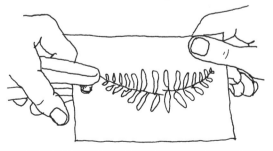

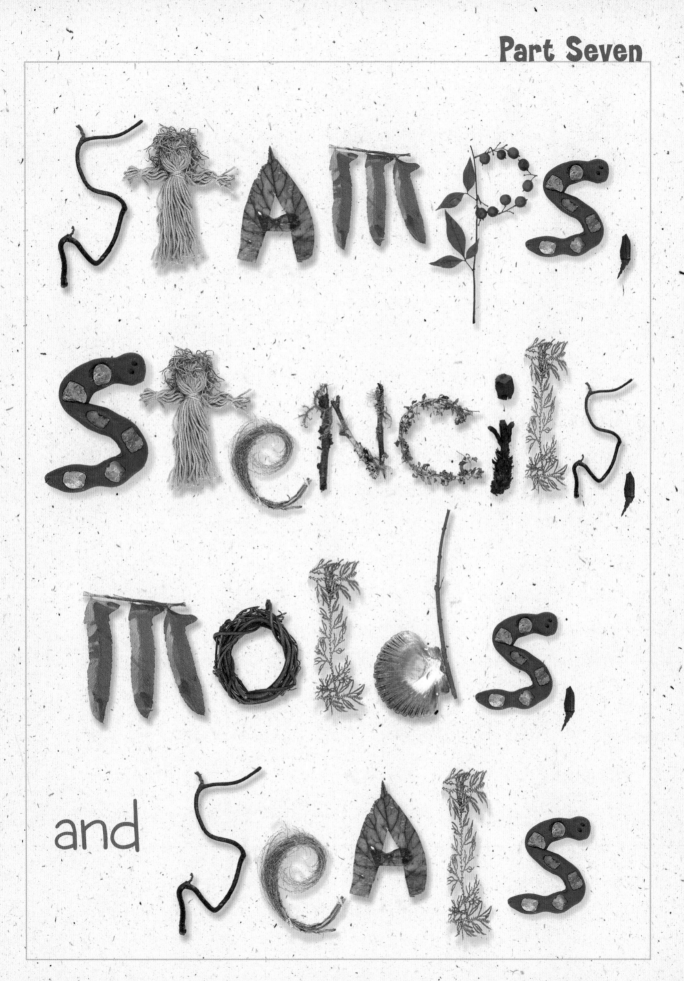

Part Seven

Stamps, Stencils, Molds, and Seals

here are many ways to use one item to make several designs. You may think that rubber stamps are a relatively new idea, but the art of putting ink onto an item that contains a raised design and transferring the design to paper is an ancient concept. You can make stamps from ferns, leaves, and flowers. For something simple, cut a design into a piece of potato, dip it into paint or ink, press it onto paper, and use the stamp over and over again (see page 174).

Nature Printing

The art of nature printing, in which the artist puts ink and paint directly onto leaves or flowers and transfers the design to paper, was popular as far back as the 16th century. In 1557, Alexis Pedemontanus wrote *The Book of Art and Nature* and said that with nature printing, "you may make gallant things to adorne your Chamber." Whether you use this craft to decorate your bedroom or make stationery or wrapping paper, you'll be amazed at the detail you get from this process.

Stencils

In addition, artists have been using stencils (cutout designs) for hundreds — if not thousands — of years to decorate fabric, paper, and walls. It is thought that the first stencils were used to decorate the Cave of a Thousand Buddhas in

Dunhuang, China, in the third century. The stencil objects we'll use for the projects in this chapter come from nature. You'll quickly learn that the most appealing stencil designs are those made with the most interesting shapes found in nature.

Seals and Sand Casting

Clay or wax seals are another way you can use one item to make several designs. Long before they could just lick and close an envelope, people secured their letters with a drop of sealing wax and then stamped the melted wax with a piece of metal inscribed with a design (called a seal). Today, we can use polymer clay instead of melted wax. Wax is brittle and can't take much wear and tear, but polymer clay can be used for many projects. You can make a great impression by pressing leaves or flowers into a small piece of clay, and you can also leave the plants in the clay as it bakes.

You can get excellent detail from nature, too, through a process called sand casting. Damp sand will hold an impression perfectly. By pouring plaster into your sand impressions, you'll create some amazing pieces of art.

PRODUCTION-LINE ART

One image — lots of designs! The idea of using the same design again and again is hardly a new one, but it's a concept that artists liked from the very beginning. Imagine, for example, an artist from olden days making a design on a pottery bowl by pressing a special leaf into it. She or he may have had to look far and wide to find just the right leaf that was just the right size and just the right shape. When the artist pressed the leaf onto the pot, it made the perfect design. Instead of throwing away the leaf and spending time looking for another, the artist used it over and over, on the same pot, on a different pot, or on another piece of art.

Making a Potato Stamp

Potatoes are great for making temporary stamps. When you slice one open, it has nice flat flesh that is easy to cut. You can cut a shape out of the potato with a knife, but it's much easier to use a small metal cookie cutter to cut out a form. Cookie cutters come in all kinds of fun and interesting shapes, including little animals. The plainer the shape, the easier it will be to recognize what the stamp looks like. As a bonus, you can make two stamps at a time — just use both halves of the potato! (This project requires adult supervision.)

You will need:

old sheet or towel

large baking potato

knife (get an adult to help you)

small metal cookie cutters

How to do it:

1 Cover your work area with a sheet or towel. Cut the potato in half lengthwise. Push a cookie cutter into the flesh side of one potato half.

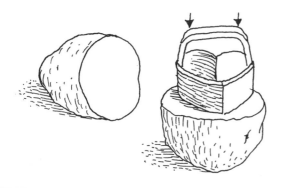

2 Leaving in the cookie cutter, use the knife to scrape away the flesh of the potato around it. Carefully remove the cookie cutter. The shape will be higher than the rest of the potato.

3 Repeat the process to make another stamp on the other half of the potato.

Potato Stamp Gift Wrap *easy*

Giving a gift you made yourself is a special thing, but wrapping it up in paper you've decorated yourself is even more special! Decorate lots of different kinds, bundle them together, and give them away as a gift.

You will need:

old sheet or towel

potato stamp (see page 174)

ink pads, acrylic or poster paints, or markers

small dish or pie plate, if needed

large piece of paper

knife, if needed (get an adult to help you)

How to do it:

1 Cover your work area with a sheet or towel. Cover the potato stamp with color from an ink pad, paint, or a marker. (If you use paint, pour a little into the dish and dip the stamp into it.)

2 Carefully print all over the paper, rolling the stamp a little to get a good image. *Note:* If you aren't getting a clear image, you may be using too much paint. If you find that other parts of the potato are picking up color and transferring it to the paper, use the knife to trim them off.

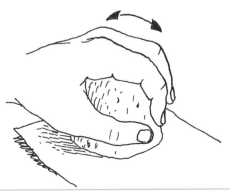

Heart Canvas Bag *easy*

Everyone loves hearts. This little bag is simple to make from scratch, or you can buy a plain bag ready-made. Either way, the bright red hearts make it come alive.

You will need:

old sheet or towel

red fabric paint or fabric marker

small dish or pie plate

heart-shaped potato stamp (see page 174)

several sheets of scrap paper

pencil, if not using ready-made canvas bag

piece of canvas 14 inches by 9 inches or ready-made canvas bag

needle and thread or sewing machine (get an adult to help you), if not using ready-made canvas bag

2 pieces of webbing, each about 12 inches long, if not using ready-made canvas bag

How to do it:

1 Cover your work area with a sheet or towel. Pour a little red fabric paint into the dish. Dip the stamp into the paint and practice stamping onto a piece of paper.

2 To make the bag, fold down the top edge of the canvas ½ inch to the inside of the bag and stitch it to make a clean edge.

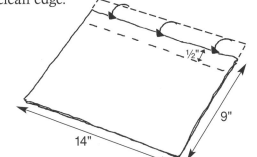

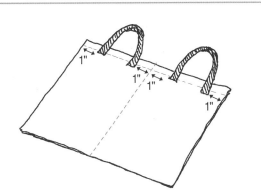

3 Fold the piece of canvas in half to find the center and mark it with a pencil. Unfold the canvas and stitch on the webbing for the handles, about 1 inch in from each side edge and middle fold.

4 Fold the piece of canvas in half (with the stitched side of the handles showing) and stitch across the bottom and up the open side. Turn right-side out.

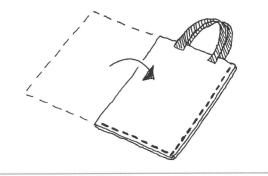

5 Put a piece of scrap paper inside the bag (to keep the paint from going through), then stamp hearts onto the outside of the bag.

Printing with Leaves

Nature provides an endless number of (free!) objects to use for printing. The idea is to put ink or paint onto the back of a leaf or flower, then press it onto paper to transfer the image. The plant material should be as flat as possible to give the cleanest image. Although some fresh plants (especially leaves) are naturally flat and can be picked and used immediately, you'll probably want to press others (see pages 160–161 to learn how to press plants). Color can come from ink pads, markers, or paint, depending on what you have available; from the colors you want and the sizes of the plants you are using.

An ink pad is the easiest way to color the back of a leaf, but most ink pads are not very large and will handle only small leaves or flowers. You can also use watercolors or markers.

You will need:

old sheet or towel

leaf for printing

ink pad, watercolors, or markers

several sheets of scrap paper

tweezers

paper for printing

small dish of soapy water (for printing with watercolors)

paintbrushes (for printing with watercolors)

How to do it:

1 Cover your work area with a sheet or towel.

2 **To print with an ink pad,** place the underside of the leaf on the ink pad. Using a piece of scrap paper, press down on the leaf until the leaf is covered with ink.

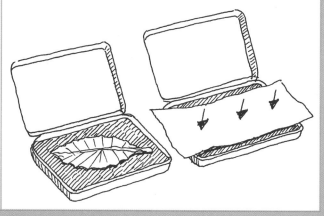

3 Remove the scrap paper and, with the tweezers, lift the leaf off the ink pad. Place it carefully on the paper you want to print. Go to step 6.

4 **To print with watercolors,** paint the underside of the leaf with soapy water, then paint it with watercolor. Use two colors, if desired. Be sure to cover the entire leaf. Place it carefully on the paper you want to print. Go to step 6.

5 **To print with markers,** apply color to the underside of the leaf. Start at the top of the leaf and work downward. Be sure to cover the entire leaf, and remember that you can use more than one color if you want to. Place it carefully on the paper you want to print.

6 Cover the leaf with a clean piece of scrap paper. Rub firmly but carefully until the ink, paint, or marker has transferred to the paper.

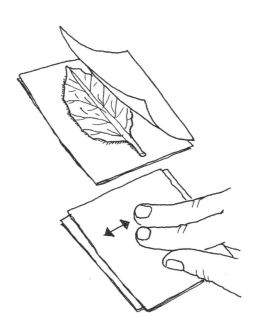

7 Remove the scrap paper. Use the tweezers to remove the leaf. Let the ink or paint dry.

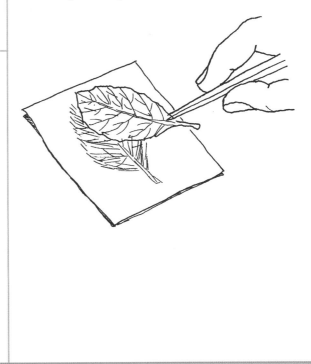

Nature Print Gift Bags medium

The idea of using a gift bag instead of wrapping up a box makes sense. A bag makes a nice-looking package and can be used again and again. This keeps people from throwing out so much wrapping paper. Making a gift bag is simple, and decorating it with nature prints is a wonderful way to make it special. This bag is flat and won't hold a lot, but it is fun to make. If you want a larger bag, buy a plain gift bag and decorate it with nature prints.

You will need:

old sheet or towel

regular envelope (any size or shape)

craft glue, if needed

ruler

scissors

hole punch

2 pieces of ribbon or raffia, each about 15 inches long

flowers or leaves

ink pad, watercolor paints, or markers

small dish of soapy water (for printing with watercolors)

paintbrushes (for printing with watercolors)

several sheets of scrap paper

tweezers

How to do it:

1 Cover your work area with a sheet or towel. Seal the envelope (just lick and seal!) or use glue, if necessary.

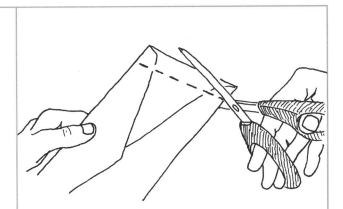

2 Turning the envelope lengthwise, use a ruler to measure ½ inch, then cut about ½ inch off one end. If the envelope is square, just cut a little bit off one end.

3 Use the hole punch to make two sets of holes about ½ inch from the top (cut) edge. Tie the ribbon through the holes for handles.

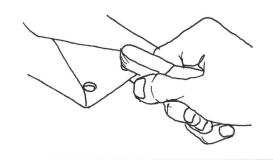

4 Practice printing the flowers or leaves with an ink pad on a piece of scrap paper to make sure your plants will work. (See the directions for printing with leaves on pages 178–179.)

5 Create a pleasing design on the bag with the plants. Print each of the flowers and leaves, following the directions on pages 178–179. After you finish, allow the ink to dry.

Nature Print Cards and Stationery medium

Mother Nature is generous in giving us so many beautiful plants we can use for printing. Look for leaves that have lots of veins on the underside, because the patterns will give you a more interesting image. Ferns are great. Also try the leaves from apple, beech, birch, dogwood, oak, poplar, sassafras, and sweet gum trees. When you've had a little practice, try printing herbs, such as lavender, oregano, and parsley. Printing with flowers is a little more difficult, but it's really not hard.

You will need:

old sheet or towel

leaves, herbs, and flowers

ink pad (one color or several colors)

scrap paper

tweezers

white or light-colored greeting cards or stationery and matching envelopes

markers, paints, or colored pencils (optional)

How to do it:

1 Cover your work area with a sheet or towel. Practice printing the leaves, herbs, and flowers with an ink pad on a piece of scrap paper to make sure your plants will work. (See the directions for printing with leaves on pages 178–179.)

2 Create a pleasing design with the plants on the front of a card or at the top or along the sides of a piece of stationery. You can use one kind of plant or different ones.

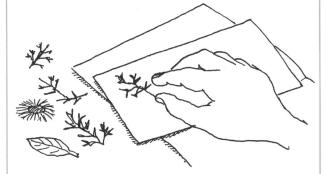

3 Print each of the leaves, herbs, and flowers, following the directions on pages 178–179. After you finish, allow the ink to dry, then use markers, paints, or colored pencils to add details and more color, if desired.

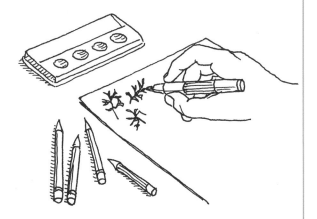

4 For an even more elegant touch, print the envelopes, too. Print on the front or across the flap on the back, putting part of the design on the top of the flap and part on the envelope.

Maybe you'd like to make a repeating design with one leaf. You can cover the entire front of a card or put a small simple design in one corner. Let your imagination and sense of design lead you.

Stenciling with Leaves and Flowers

Nature is full of interesting shapes that you can use as stencils. Leaves are the easiest things to use, but ferns and flowers are good, too. To get a really sharp stencil, the plant should be flat and stay perfectly still. If you need to, press the plant for a day or two (see page 161) before you use it.

You will need:

old sheet or towel

acrylic paints, poster paints, or watercolors

small dish or pie plate

double-sided tape or regular tape

flat, broad, interestingly shaped leaves

plain newsprint from a craft-supply store

sponge

tweezers

How to do it:

1 Cover your work area with a sheet or towel. Pour some paint into a small dish.

2 Place a piece of double-sided tape on a leaf and stick it to a piece of newsprint. (Regular tape will work fine if you fold it over so that it sticks to itself.) Use more than one piece of tape, if necessary. Make sure the tape does not go past the edge of the leaf. If it does, use a larger leaf.

3 Dip the sponge into the paint and carefully sponge around the leaf, covering all the edges. Be careful not to get paint underneath the leaf.

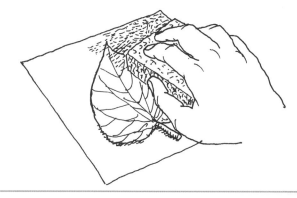

4 Use tweezers to remove the leaf. You should see paint everywhere except where the leaf was.

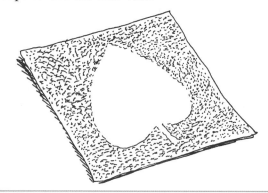

5 Move the leaf to another spot or use a different leaf, taped in the same way, and repeat steps 3 and 4 until you have covered the paper. Let the paint dry.

Leaf Rubbing Gift Wrap *easy*

If you want a quick way to make leaf prints, simply rub the crayons over the leaves wherever you like. If you take the time to mark off squares, you can create a very beautiful, professional-looking piece of wrapping paper.

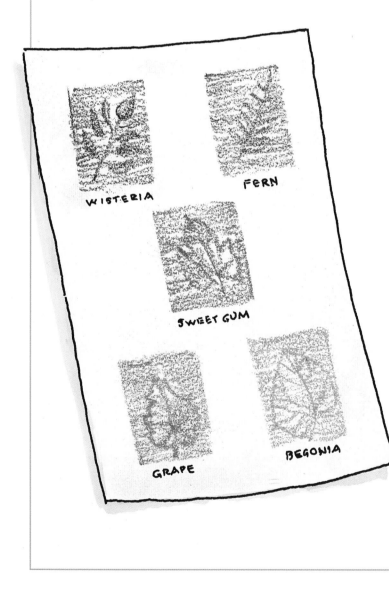

You will need:

old sheet or towel

leaves with lots of veins

plain newsprint from a craft-supply store

crayons

removable tape (optional)

How to do it:

1 Cover your work area with a sheet or towel. Place a leaf, vein-side up, on a smooth surface.

2 Place the newsprint over the leaf and rub with a crayon, until the shape and veins in the leaf appear. Don't rub too hard, or you'll flatten the veins in the leaf. Repeat with other leaves until you have covered the paper with different rubbings.

3 If you want neat squares around your leaves, put removable tape in a square around each leaf. The crayon marks will not show up where the tape is, giving you a nice clean edge.

Fern Stencil Box

challenging

Many plants you'll want for your stencils are not wide enough to use with adhesive tape, but there is a trick to keep your favorite plants in place while you paint around them. Although ancient artists didn't have this option, you can use an old pair of panty hose to secure the plants. Spray paint will go through the panty hose but not the plant, giving you a good stencil design. *Note: Choose a nice day for this project; you'll be doing part of it outside!* (This project requires adult supervision.)

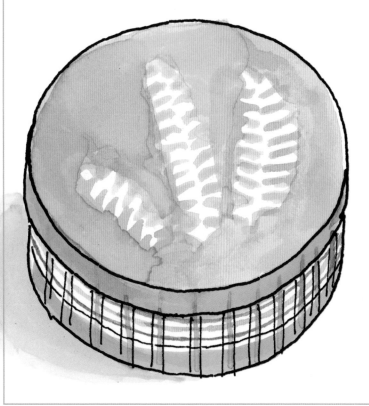

STENCIL SHAPES

To make a stencil in any shape, take a piece of poster board and draw a design on it — for example, a heart. Make a slit along the outline of the heart so you can stick the tip of your scissors through, then carefully cut out the heart without touching the rest of the board. Now you have two hearts — one that is a hole and one that is an object. You can use either one as a stencil, filling in the heart hole or coloring around the heart object.

How to do it:

1 Cover your work area with a sheet or towel. Place the ferns in a pleasing design on the top of the box. Carefully pull the panty hose over the box, working with your hands inside the hose to keep the ferns in place. Pull the panty hose tightly over the box and secure it on the bottom with string or twistie ties.

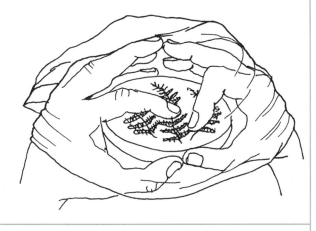

2 Take the newspapers outside and lay them out to give yourself a good work surface. Carefully take out the box, lay it on top of the newspapers with the fern side facing up, and spray-paint the top of the box. Make sure the force of the spray doesn't move the ferns. Let the paint dry.

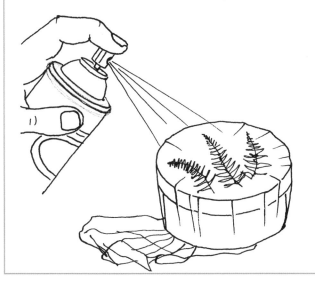

3 Remove the panty hose and the ferns and voilà! — a perfect fern design on the box.

4 If you want, spray-paint the sides of the box or repeat steps 1 through 3 with other ferns.

5 Cover the rim of the box top with ribbon, if desired. Wrap the ribbon around the edge so you know how long it should be, cut it to the correct length with scissors, and glue it to the edge.

Here are some other ideas for using stamped or stenciled images:

◉ binder cover

◉ gift tag

◉ picture frame cover

◉ framed art

◉ personalized stationery

Flower-and-Leaf Barrette, Pin, or Magnet *easy*

Leaves and flowers pressed into pieces of clay and then baked make beautiful little gift items. (This project requires adult supervision.)

You will need:

old sheet or towel

white polymer clay

plastic wrap

rolling pin

pressed leaves and flowers

plastic knife

baking sheet

aluminum foil

paintbrush

clear polymer clay glaze

craft glue

barrette clip, jewelry pin, or magnet

How to do it:

1 Cover your work area with a sheet or towel. Preheat the oven to 275°F.

2 Put the clay between pieces of plastic wrap and roll it out flat to about ¼ inch thick.

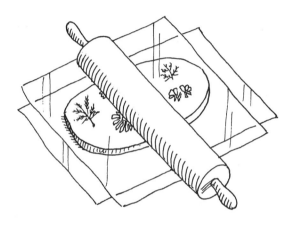

3 Remove plastic wrap and firmly press your leaves and flowers into the clay. Cover them again with plastic wrap and press them into the clay with a rolling pin.

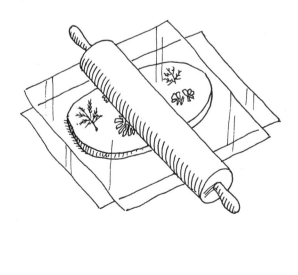

4 With the knife, cut the clay into the desired shapes. (The barrette is slightly larger than the metal barrette clip, which is about 2 inches long and ¾ inch across; small jewelry pins and magnets are 1 to 2 inches across.)

5 Place the clay on the baking sheet lined with foil. Bake for 6 to 8 minutes or until hard.

6 Remove from the oven and cool. When the pieces are cool, brush on the polymer clay glaze.

7 When the glaze is dry, glue the barrette clip, jewelry pin, or magnet to the back of the clay. Make sure you glue the clip or pin in the correct direction, so that when you wear the piece it is right-side up.

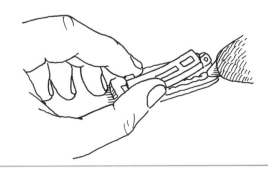

Clay Fossil *easy*

Fossils are traces of ancient plants and animals that have been preserved in the earth. Some fossils show the outline of these creatures clearly, and with other fossils you can barely see them, because the impressions have been worn away — eroded — by time and weather. When you make your own fossils, you'll take an impression of leaves or shells in clay and then bake the clay to make the impression permanent. Just like real fossils, some of these will be distinct and others will be kind of difficult to see. See pages 84–85 to learn how to make statues and animal fetishes out of clay and page 81 for how to bake polymer clay. (This project requires adult supervision.)

You will need:

old sheet or towel

white polymer clay

plastic wrap

rolling pin

leaf, shell, cone — any treasure that will give a good impression

tweezers, if needed

plastic knife

baking sheet

aluminum foil

paintbrush (optional)

clear polymer clay glaze (optional)

How to do it:

1 Cover your work area with a sheet or towel. Preheat the oven to 275°F.

2 Put the clay between pieces of plastic wrap and roll it out flat to about ¼ inch thick.

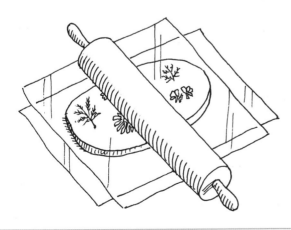

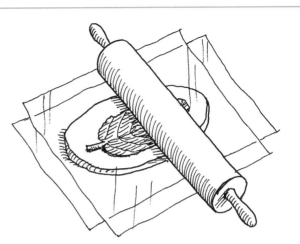

3 Remove plastic wrap and firmly press your treasure into the clay. Cover the clay and the treasure with plastic wrap and use the rolling pin to gently flatten the clay.

4 Remove the treasure from the clay, using the tweezers, if necessary. With the knife, cut the clay into the desired shape.

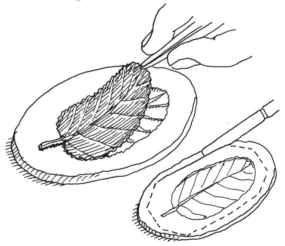

5 Place the clay on a baking sheet lined with foil. Bake for 8 to 10 minutes, or until hard.

6 Remove from the oven and cool. When the piece is cool, paint it with the polymer glaze, if desired.

Clay Wall Hanging *easy*

Decorated tiles or plaques have always been used as pieces of art. Although when you buy these in the store, they are very expensive, you can make your own for very little money.
(This project requires adult supervision.)

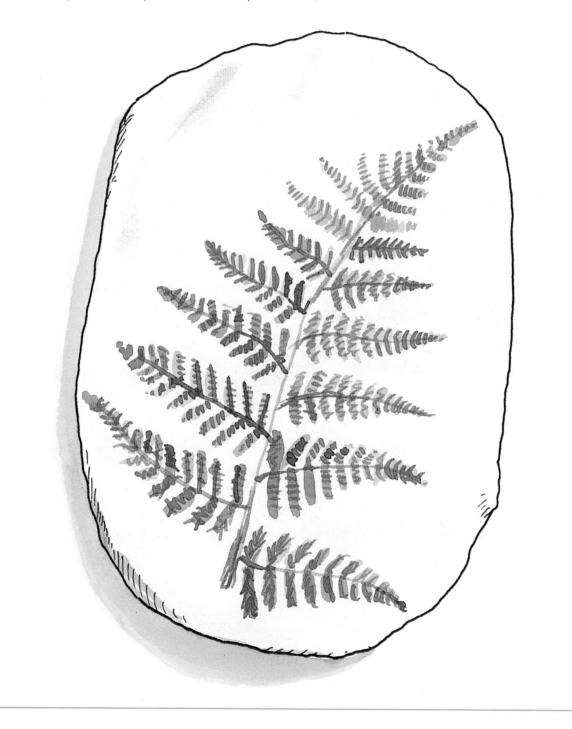

You will need:

old sheet or towel

white polymer clay

plastic wrap

rolling pin

fern

plastic knife

baking sheet

aluminum foil

paintbrush

clear polymer clay glaze

craft glue or glue gun and glue sticks (see Glue Gun Caution! on page 7)

metal hanger

Use flowers or leaves instead of the fern. Add pieces of fern or twigs to make your wall hanging even more exciting.

How to do it:

1 Cover your work area with a sheet or towel. Preheat the oven to 275°F.

2 Put the clay between pieces of plastic wrap and roll it out flat to about ¼ inch thick. Press the fern into the clay.

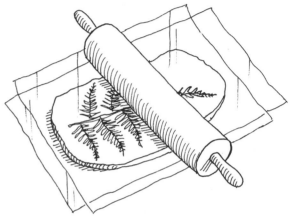

3 Use the knife to neaten the edges or cut the clay to the desired size and shape.

4 Place the clay on a baking sheet lined with foil. Bake for about 8 minutes, or until hard.

5 Remove from the oven and cool. When the piece has cooled, paint it with the polymer glaze. When the glaze is dry, glue the hanger to the back.

Sand-Cast Paperweight medium

Have you ever built a sand castle? If so, you know what a great material sand is to work with. In this craft, we're making shapes and holes in the sand rather than building it up. If you get the sand just wet enough — but not too wet — it will keep the exact shape of anything you put into it. But what good is nicely shaped sand? Not much, for it will soon dry out and collapse. But as long as the shape is there, you can pour in a substance such as metal or plaster that will, in turn, take on the shape of the mold. Because peach pits have such an interesting texture, they make unique designs for sand molds. (This project requires adult supervision.)

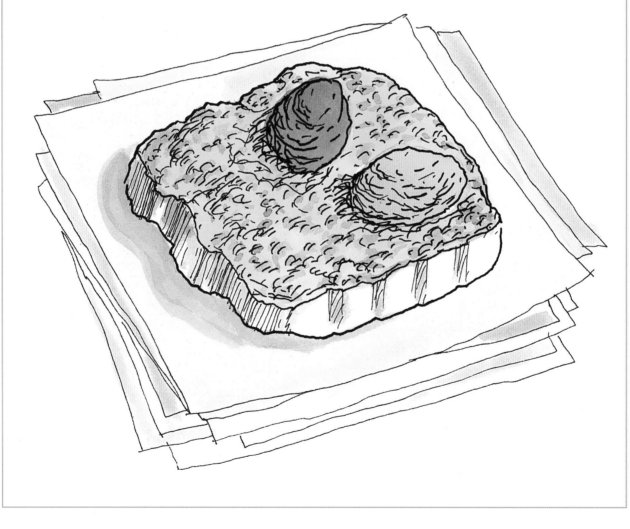

You will need:

old sheet or towel

sand

large bowl

small square disposable container

2 or 3 peach pits

long wooden spoon or stick

plaster of Paris

disposable bowl or container

paintbrush

reddish brown watercolor or acrylic paint

scissors

foam, for backing

craft glue

How to do it:

1 Cover your work area with a sheet or towel. Place the sand in a bowl and moisten it with water until it is the right consistency. It must be firm to the touch but able to keep a perfect impression.

2 Place the sand in the square disposable container. Carefully push two or three peach pits (or the same pit two or three times) into the sand to make a mold. If you push the pits about halfway down into the sand, they should make a good mold. Carefully remove the pits.

3 Using the spoon, mix the plaster in the disposable bowl, following the package directions. Make sure the plaster pours easily but is not too thin. Pour the plaster into the sand mold and let dry thoroughly.

4 Pull the plaster away from the sand and brush off any sand with your hands. When the plaster has hardened, brush on some reddish brown paint to look like real peach pits.

5 To turn your artwork into a paperweight, cut a piece of foam the same size as the bottom of the plaster mold, then glue it on. Now your paperweight will stay put when you use it!

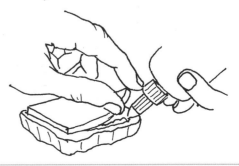

Sand-Cast Sea Treasure medium

Shells, starfish, sea creatures — all make beautiful shapes in sand, and they look quite natural in sand-casted items, as if you have frozen a piece of the bottom of the sea. (This project requires adult supervision.)

old sheet or towel

sand

large bowl

medium-sized container, such as a plastic food tray, large enough to pack at least a 2-inch-deep layer of sand

sea treasures (shells, starfish)

long wooden spoon or stick

plaster of Paris

disposable bowl or container

watercolor or acrylic paint

paintbrush

scissors

foam, for backing (optional)

craft glue

hook (optional)

How to do it:

1 Cover your work area with a sheet or towel. Place the sand in a bowl and moisten it with water until it is the right consistency. It must be firm to the touch but able to keep a perfect impression.

2 Place at least a 2-inch-deep layer of sand in the container (deeper if you are using a large treasure). Carefully push the treasure into the sand to make a mold. If you push it about halfway down into the sand, it should make a good mold. Carefully remove the treasure.

3 Using the spoon, mix the plaster in the disposable bowl, following the package directions. Make sure the plaster pours easily but is not too thin. Pour the plaster into the sand mold and let dry thoroughly.

4 Pull the plaster away from the sand, brush off any sand with your hands, and paint the plaster.

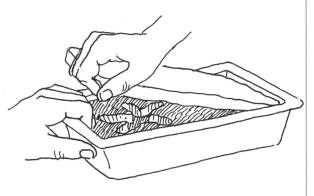

5 If you'd like to hang your piece of art, cut a piece of foam the same size as the bottom of the mold and glue it on. Then glue a hook onto the foam for hanging.

nature skills

Wherever you live, you can find treasures in nature. The trick is to go outside, look around, and use your imagination. The charts on pages 200–211 will give you a quick overview of some of the many wonderful things you can find in nature to use in crafts. As you look for treasures and become more fascinated by the natural world, you'll probably want to refer to more complete identification guides. Choose guides that have good pictures as well as clear information to help you identify the plants, rocks, and shells that you find.

Vines

Vines are plants that put out long stems so they can creep along the ground or climb over trees. Be careful — some vines, such as poison ivy, are *not* friendly.

What	Where and When	How to Use
Grapevine There are many kinds of grapevines. They have curly little stems called *tendrils* that are very attractive in crafts.	Some sort of grape grows in almost all parts of the U.S. and Canada. Grapevines can be harvested almost anytime. The vines may not be strong enough to use in early spring, however.	Excellent for weaving into wreaths (see pages 16–17) and baskets (see pages 22–23). Use leaves for nature printing, pressing, hammering, and rubbing (see pages 106–109, 130, 160–161, and 178–179).
Honeysuckle A vine that stays at least partially evergreen in warmer regions. It grows very quickly and can be a real pest in the garden; however, the flowers smell wonderful.	Throughout the U.S. and Canada. White and gold flowers appear in late spring and throughout the summer.	Excellent for weaving into wreaths (see pages 16–17) and baskets (see pages 22–23). Use leaves for nature printing, pressing, hammering, and rubbing (see pages 106–109, 130, 160–161, and 178–179).
Virginia Creeper (woodbine) A woodland plant that puts out long stems along the ground, called *runners*. It has attractive dark green leaves that come in fives. *Note:* This looks something like poison ivy, except that poison ivy has only three leaves. Make sure you harvest the vine that has *five* leaves, the Virginia creeper. If you're not sure, ask for help in identifying the right vine.	Forests throughout the eastern U.S. Best harvested during summer. Look for long runners.	In weaving and basket making (see pages 16–17 and 22–23).

Trees

There are two classes of trees: **needle-leaved** trees and **broad-leaved** trees. Needle-leaved trees have leaves so narrow that they are called needles (like those on a pine tree). The needles stay on the tree year-round. These trees are called **evergreens.** Broad-leaved trees have flat, broad leaves (such as a maple tree and an oak tree). The leaves drop in fall (and most of them change colors before they drop). These are called **deciduous** trees.

What	Where and When	How to Use
Birch Tall tree (40–100 feet) with beautiful bark. The bark is light colored, sometimes white or ash (light grayish cream), with black lines going around the tree. The leaves are 2 to 3 inches long with toothed edges.	Deciduous forests throughout the U.S. and Canada. Leaves turn golden yellow in fall.	Twigs and branches for any twig project (see pages see bottom of page); fallen bark for covering baskets (see pages 40–41) or making elf houses (see pages 44–51).
Oak Huge (30–100 feet), deciduous tree. There are 450 species of oaks.	Forests throughout the U.S. and Canada. Leaves turn bronze or deep red in fall.	Thin slices, called splints, are used to make baskets (see pages 22–23). Use twigs and branches for any twig craft (see pages 24–49, 62–63, 92–93, and 156); use leaves for pressing, nature printing, and rubbing (see pages 130, 160–161, and 178–179).
Raffia Palm A tree that produces leaves that are terrific for doing a wide variety of crafts. The leaves are dried and shredded into long, cordlike strings.	The plant grows on the island of Madagascar, off the southeast coast of Africa, but the commercial product, raffia, can be found at any craft store. Grows throughout the year.	Great for tying things together, making bows, and adorning wreaths (see pages 22–23, 28–32, 34–35, 60–61, 64–69, 86–87, and 154–155); or braided into long strands and coiled to create baskets (see pages 21–23).
Sassafras Slender tree with one of three types of leaves. They are either oval, have three fingers, or look like a mitten. Grows as tall as 50 feet.	Deciduous forests in the eastern U.S. and Canada. Leaves turn red in fall.	Twigs and branches in any twig project (see pages 24–49, 62–63, 92–93, and 156); leaves for nature printing, rubbing, and pressing (see pages 130, 160–161, and 178–179).
Yucca There are many kinds of yucca. Most have strong, sword-shaped leaves and produce a stalk of white, bell-shaped flowers. Be careful, because some of these leaves can cut you.	Different types grow in various places, from the deserts to the coasts. Harvest leaves and roots year-round.	Weaving material (see pages 22–23).

Vegetables and Herbs

Although most vegetables and herbs are grown for eating and flavoring, many are also great to use in crafts. These are just some suggestions — use your imagination to come up with other ideas.

What	Where and When	How to Use
Corn Actually a grass grown for the ears, which have seeds, called *kernels*. The name *corn* can be a little confusing to some people, because in England, *corn* means wheat. In Scotland and Ireland, it means oats. In the British Isles, their word *maize* is our word *corn*. There are many kinds of corn, including popcorn and decorative red and purple Indian corn, also called maize!	In vegetable gardens in summer and in supermarkets year-round. For craft purposes, get corn with the husks still on or purchase just the husks (these are sold in supermarkets for making Mexican tamales).	Use husks for weaving and making hats, baskets, and dolls (see pages 28–32, 42–43, 52–53, and 64–69).
Gourds Bizarre-looking vegetables that you can't eat. They come in odd shapes and textures — some are very hard, some have warty shells, others are smooth and soft-skinned. They are hollow inside. They are named for what they look like, such as the serpent gourd, the spoon gourd, and the caveman's club gourd.	In vegetable gardens in fall.	Paint smooth-shelled gourds (see pages 58–59); leave seeds in to make rattles (see pages 60–61).
Okra A tall summer vegetable with beautiful flowers. The fruit is tasty, but the texture takes some getting used to, as it is hairy on the outside. Gumbo, a southern stew, often includes okra. If left on the plant, it develops into large, hard seedpods that are really pretty.	In vegetable gardens in warm regions. It loves hot weather. Allow seedpods to ripen in late summer or early fall. Also, some craft stores carry okra pods in their dried-flower departments.	Seedpods make good decorations (see pages 62–63).
Rosemary An herb with a great smell, something like pine. It has needlelike leaves and is used to flavor food.	In herb gardens in full sun. Harvest long stems in summer and early fall.	For making potpourri (see page 134); long stems can be woven into wreaths (see pages 16–17).

Plants for Coloring and Painting

You can use many kinds of plants to make color for your art, even if you live in the city. The following list provides ideas to start with, but you don't need to stop there. Keep exploring the world of plants. Remember not to pick more than you're going to use. If you do find yourself with extra plants, though, place them in a plastic bag and put them into the refrigerator until you need them again.

What	Where and When	How to Use
Aster A great plant that is both a wild-flower and a garden flower and can be bought from a florist. Most asters have small purple flowers that look like little daisies; some are white or pink. Grows 3–5 feet tall.	Along roadsides and in flower gardens. Most bloom in fall.	**For hammering.** Aster hammers fairly well, but the purple color often turns brown. **For pressing.** Press individual flowers and some leaves and stems.
Cabbage, red Vegetable with dark reddish purple leaves. Grows 10–12 inches across.	In vegetable gardens in summer and at super-markets year-round. Choose a head with the most colorful leaves possible.	**As a dye.** Pull apart the cabbage head. *Note:* This is a great job for young children. Breaking up the cabbage is not messy, won't hurt them if they eat it (on the contrary!), and is fun to do. Separate the leaves and break them into small pieces. Place the torn leaves in a small pot and cover with water. Place the pot on the stove and set the heat on low. Simmer 1–2 hours, or until the leaves lose their color. *Caution:* Do not burn. Cool and strain out leaves. Makes a delightful purplish blue.
Carrot Tops Bright green frilly leaves on the tops of an orange root vegetable. Tops usually measure 6–8 inches long.	In vegetable gardens in spring and early summer and at super-markets year-round.	**For hammering.** Spread out the individual leaves, making sure a little space remains between each piece. **As a dye.** Gather several bunches of carrot tops and place them in a large bowl. Cover with water and set in a sunny place for a couple of days, then pour the water and carrot tops into a large pot. Place the pot on the stove and set the heat on low. Simmer for 30–40 minutes, or until green color comes out of the leaves. Strain off the plant material.
Chrysanthemum Beautiful plant with flowers in yellow, white, pink, red, orange, purple, and rust. Varies in height; most are 2–4 feet tall. Garden flowers are often taller.	In flower gardens in fall and flower shops year-round.	**As a dye.** See pages 122–126. **For pressing.** Flowers with a single row of petals work best. Remove each petal and press separately.

continued →

Plants for Coloring and Painting

What	Where and When	How to Use
Coreopsis Bright yellow flower with dark green leaves. Grows 3 feet tall. Blossoms are 1½ inches across.	In sunny gardens and along roadsides in summer.	**For hammering.** Clip off the stem just below the blossom head. Place it "sunny-side down" on the material to be hammered. Tape all the petals, then cut off the green parts. Remove any extra material from the center, leaving just the petals. **As a dye.** Place several cups of blossoms in a large pot and add water to cover. Place the pot on the stove and bring to a boil. Lower the heat and simmer, uncovered, for 30–60 minutes. Strain off the plant material.
Cosmos Tall plant with large pink, dark pink, or white flowers (white flowers won't hammer). The petals are notched on the ends; the leaves are fernlike. Grows 4 feet tall.	In sunny gardens in summer.	**For hammering.** Clip off a single blossom. Remove as much of the center as you can without tearing up the flower. Place it colorful-side down to hammer.
Dahlia Beautiful garden plant with large, brightly colored blossoms of yellow, orange, red, white, cream, and pink. Although you can buy dwarf varieties that are not taller than about 16 inches, most dahlias are large plants growing 3–4 feet tall.	In sunny gardens in late spring, summer, and into fall.	**For hammering.** Pick off petals and assemble on paper or fabric one at a time. Tape down and hammer. Create a circular flower shape with many petals. **As a dye.** Pick off flowers and place in a large pot. Cover with water. Simmer on the stove for 30–45 minutes, until the water is colored, then strain off the plant material. Do not allow the temperature to get too high or the colors will look brown.
Dianthus (carnation family) Bushy little plant, whose flower petals are notched on the ends. Comes in pink, red, red and white, and solid white. Grows 1½ feet tall.	In flower gardens in spring and summer and at flower shops and supermarkets year-round.	**For hammering.** Spread out the petals, clip off any extra plant material from the back, and hammer. Dianthus petals almost always turn a purplish color. If you use carnations, pull out individual petals and arrange them on your material as you wish, then hammer.
Dill Tall, frilly-leaved herb that smells great when you crush the leaves. The leaves are long and narrow and cut into many segments. The blossom is flat and yellow and about 8 inches across. Usually grows 2–5 feet tall.	In herb gardens in summer and at supermarkets year-round.	**For hammering.** Choose leaves that are not very full. Spread out each individual piece of leaf; don't bunch them.
Dusty Miller Plant grown for its interesting gray-green leaves, which have round scallops called *lobes*. Grows about 2½ feet tall.	In sunny flower gardens in summer. Leaves are plentiful in summer, though they last well into fall in warmer areas.	**For hammering.** Whitish gray leaves turn green when hammered and make a great shape. **For pressing.** Very good plant to press, because of the interesting shape of the leaves.

Plants for Coloring and Painting

What	Where and When	How to Use
Fern There are many kinds of ferns. Some are very tall, some have huge *fronds* (which is what fern leaves are called), and some have tiny hairlike fronds. (Asparagus fern, with bright green frilly leaves, is not really a fern, according to scientists, but it looks like a fern, so lots of people call it that.) They vary in size from a couple of inches tall to tree ferns that grow very large.	Ferns generally like shady areas under trees; many like moist spots, too, such as beside a stream. In nature, you'll find the most number of ferns during summer. Some ferns, in some parts of the country, stay green all year. Because ferns also make good houseplants, you can find them at nurseries and flower shops.	**For hammering.** Most ferns are great to hammer, particularly on cloth. Place with the brownish side down, separating each piece and taping it down. **As a dye.** Bracken fern is good for making a green dye. Cut up a large grocery bagful of bracken fern. Soak overnight in a large bowl. Place in a pot and simmer on the stove for 1 hour, then strain out the plant material. This makes a nice soft green dye.
Goldenrod Different types of goldenrod grow in various parts of the U.S., but almost all have bright yellow plumes of flowers with long, narrow leaves. Grows 1–5 feet tall.	In fields and along roadsides in late summer and fall.	**As a dye.** Pluck off the flower heads and try to use only the yellow parts. Place in a pot, cover with water, and simmer on the stove for 1 hour. Strain out the plant material.
Hydrangea Shrub with big flower heads of pink, blue, or white. Grows 4–8 feet tall.	At the edge of woods or underneath trees in early summer.	**For drying.** Wait to pick until the flowers begin to feel a little papery on the shrub. Dry by standing the stalks upright in a vase or bottle without water. **For pressing.** Press individual flowers.
Impatiens Short little plants with blossoms that have five rounded petals. They come in pink, purple, red, white, and orange, with small, light green leaves. Grows to 1½ feet tall.	In shady gardens and pots in summer.	**For hammering.** Turn over the flower and you'll see a small spur. Use your fingernail to clip this off. Place the brighter side down and hammer. The leaves sometimes squish out, so hammer gently at first. These colors will fade quickly. *Note:* An individual pink petal makes a great face for a figure.
Ivy There are many kinds of ivy, but the most common is English ivy, which is a creeping vine with leaves that have 3–5 points on them. Older leaves are dark green with white veins. Younger leaves are light yellow or green. When growing along the ground, it gets only a few inches tall. When it grows up trees or buildings, the vines can grow 15–20 feet and more.	In shady gardens and woods and along roadsides.	**For hammering.** Only the young, fresh leaves will hammer well. You must hammer ivy on cloth. It does not work well on paper. **As a dye.** Fill a grocery bag half full of leaves, put them into a medium-sized pot, cover with water, and place the pot in a warm, sunny spot for a couple of days. Place the pot, with the leaves still in it, on the stove and bring to a boil, then quickly turn the heat to low and simmer for 1–2 hours, until color comes out of the leaves.

continued →

Plants for Coloring and Painting

What	Where and When	How to Use
Juniper Evergreen plant that grows either close to the ground or tall, like a shrub. It has needlelike foliage (like short pine needles). Usually grows 1–5 feet tall. Some are treelike and can reach 20 feet in height.	In gardens and woods.	**For hammering.** Spread out the needles in a single layer, leaving space between the needles. Hammer with enthusiasm. **As a dye.** Gather ripe juniper berries. These will be silver-blue. Place them in a large tub of water for several days. Crush the berries as they soften. Pour into medium-sized pot. Place the pot on the stove and boil on medium high for about 20 minutes. Do not allow the berries to burn. Let cool. Strain off the berries.
Lichen Combination of a fungus and an alga. Fungi do not have green leaves and must live off other organisms. Algae are green and can make food but have no roots. The two plants make a perfect team. Most woodland lichen is black, gray-green, or light yellow-green. Grows on rocks and stones, logs, twigs, and the bark of trees. Some are flat, some curly, and some look like light green hair. Vary in size.	In the woods and at the seashore year-round.	Great for woodland projects (see pages 34–35). **As a dye.** Place a layer of lichen on the bottom of a pot. Place mordanted wool or cotton on top of this (see page 123). Layer more lichen, more cloth, then more lichen. Pour water over all. Place the pot on the stove and gently boil on medium high for a couple of hours; do not stir. Remove from the heat and leave the lichen and the cloth in the pot. Let cool for 24 hours. Pull out the cloth and shake off any extra lichen pieces. Rinse well.
Lobelia Garden plant with bright blue blossoms on slender stems with narrow leaves. Grows about 12 inches tall.	In gardens. Blooms in spring in hot regions, in summer in cooler areas.	**For hammering.** Clip the small green parts off the backs of the petals and spread apart the two upper petals and the three lower ones. If you can get only the lower petals, that's okay; the upper ones aren't necessary.
Maple There are many kinds of maple leaves, but the smaller, Japanese maples are best for crafts. Some maples grow really big — 60–80 feet tall. Japanese maples are usually much smaller, some reaching only 2–3 feet in height.	In forests, along city streets, in gardens, and in parks. Leaves are on the trees from spring through early fall.	**For hammering.** Japanese maples will hammer when they are in their bright fall colors, but often they are too dry for this technique. Young spring leaves hammer well. Place them vein side facedown on cloth (it will not work on paper). Tape down and hammer with enthusiasm.
Marigold Old-fashioned flower with blossoms of yellow, red, or orange. Leaves are bright green and finely cut. Grows 6–36 inches tall.	In sunny gardens in summer.	**For hammering.** Pull petals off the flower and place them in a circle on your material. Tape down to keep them in place, then hammer. Some marigolds will change to an unattractive brown when hammered. Try hammering on a piece of cloth that has been treated with a mordant (see page 123). **As a dye.** Empty a bagful of blossoms into a flat-bottomed pot. Use only the colorful petals, and tear apart the blossoms. Cover with water. Place the pot on the stove and simmer for 1 hour. Cool, then strain out the plant material.

Plants for Coloring and Painting

What	Where and When	How to Use
Onion Vegetable eaten for its round root. Choose ones with lots of skin, which comes in either purple or brown. Most onions are 2–6 inches across.	In vegetable gardens in spring and summer and at supermarkets year-round.	**As a dye.** Peel the colored skins off the onion. Purple and brown onions both make a brown dye. Ask at the grocery store whether they have extra skins you can take home. Put the skins into a medium-sized pot and cover with water. Place the pot on the stove and bring to a boil, then quickly turn down the heat to low and simmer for 1 hour, adding water if you need more liquid. Strain out the skins.
Pelargonium (geranium) Brightly colored garden plant with blossoms of white, coral, red, pink, or red and white. Leaves are rounded with curly edges. Grows 2 feet tall.	In gardens, pots, and hanging baskets in summer.	**For hammering.** Take apart the individual flowers and put them back together, taped down, on your material.
Primrose Flower with bright yellow, blue, white, or red blossoms. Grows 8 inches tall.	In shade gardens in early spring; most varieties are available as houseplants in nurseries in early spring.	**For hammering.** Clip blossoms off stem. Place the colorful side down and hammer gently. **For pressing.** Pick flowers and snip off the green stem and *sepals* (green parts just below the petals). Make sure the petals are laid out flat. Press crinkly leaves as well.
Rose One of the most beautiful garden plants; produces stunning flowers on prickly shrubs. Garden shrubs grow from tiny (less than 6 inches tall) to huge (more than 6 feet tall). Climbing varieties grow over arbors, fences, and trellises.	In sunny gardens in late spring through early fall and as a cut flower at flower shops year-round.	**For pressing.** Roses with only a single row of petals can be pressed flat. Others should be taken apart and pressed one petal at a time. **For drying.** Pick roses in bud or slightly opened, then hang them upside down in a cool, dry place.
Tansy Weedy herb with bright yellow, buttonlike blossoms and a strong smell. Grows up to 3 feet tall.	In herb gardens, along roadsides, and in fields in summer; flowers are best gathered in late summer or early fall.	**As a dye.** Gather bagsfuls of the yellow blossoms. Place the blossoms in a medium-sized pot, and cover with water. Place the pot on the stove and boil for 1 hour. Add more water if you need more liquid. Strain off the plant material.
Vinca Garden plant with five petals and shiny dark green leaves. The flowers may be deep pink, purplish pink, pink and white, or all white. There is also a blue vinca, a vine that blooms in spring. Grows 8–12 inches tall.	In sunny gardens and as edging around trees in summer.	**For hammering.** Put the colorful side down, clip off the little white tube on the back, and tape down the petals before you hammer.

continued →

Plants for Coloring and Painting

What	Where and When	How to Use
Viola and Pansy Great plants to grow for many crafts. Violas look like small pansies. Viola and pansy blossoms come in white, purple, blue, yellow, and sometimes pink. Each has five petals. Viola blossoms are less than 1 inch across; pansy blossoms can be several inches across. Both grow 6–8 inches tall.	In gardens in cool weather; spring in all areas, fall in warmer regions.	**For hammering.** These are excellent flowers to hammer. Turn them facedown on your material. Carefully tape down all the petals, then clip off the green parts. Cover with a paper towel and hammer gently but thoroughly. **For pressing.** Clip the stem off a blossom and press separately. *Note:* Colors tend to fade after a few months.
Walnut, black Nuts from the walnut tree; ripen in October or November. The tree grows 70–90 feet tall; the nuts measure about 2 inches across.	In woodlands throughout the eastern half of the U.S. and in Canada, too. Grown elsewhere in orchards.	**As a dye.** Put the outer shells into a large bowl or pot. Cover with water and let soak for a day or two. Pour the water and shells into a medium-sized pot. Place the pot on the stove and bring to a boil, then quickly turn the heat to low and simmer for a couple of hours. You can either turn off the heat and continue to soak the shells for a deeper dye or for an ink or strain off the husks and use the dye right away. *Note:* If you are allergic to walnuts, be careful working with them. Wash your hands carefully after you are done, and wash all utensils, pots, and equipment before anyone uses them for cooking or preparing food.
Zinnia Garden plant with blossoms of pink, red, yellow, orange, cream, or lavender. Grows 1–3 feet tall.	In sunny gardens in summer.	**For hammering.** Take the petals off the flower one at a time. Place them in a circle on your material (paper will not work), tape them in place, and hammer. **As a dye.** Fill a small saucepan half full with blossoms. Place the saucepan on the stove and bring to a boil, then quickly turn the heat to low and simmer for ½–1 hour. Cool, then strain out the plant material.

ZINNIA seeds

Flowers for Drying

Some flowers are better for drying than others. Below is a list of the best ones. Hydrangea and rose are also excellent; they are featured on pages 205 and 207. See page 160 for flowers that are good for pressing.

What	Where and When	How to Use
Baby's Breath Shrublike plant with frilly white flowers often used by flower shops. Cut-flower stems are 12–18 inches tall.	In flower gardens in summer; at flower shops year-round.	For dried-flower crafts. This is one of the easiest plants to dry. Pick the flowers when they are fully opened. Stand them upright in a vase with either no water or a small amount of water.
Cockscomb Garden plant with two distinctly different flowers. One looks like a grain with rows of flowers; the other is a tall, slender, fan-shaped blossom. Both come in shades of pink, orange, red, and yellow. Grows 1½–2 feet tall.	In flower gardens in summer.	For dried-flower crafts; hang upside down in a cool, dry place.
Globe Amaranth Plant with papery-feeling, ball-shaped flower heads in white, red, or purplish pink. Grows 9–12 inches tall.	In sunny gardens in summer.	For dried-flower crafts; pick the flowers when they are fully opened and abundant, then hang them in bunches upside down in a cool, dry place.
Larkspur Flower with tall spikes of purple, blue, or pink blossoms. Grows 2–5 feet tall.	In sunny gardens in late spring, before the weather gets too hot.	For dried-flower crafts; pick anytime during the growing season; the buds are as pretty as the flowers. Hang in bundles upside down in a cool, dry place.
Lavender Shrubby plant with gray-green leaves and spikes of fragrant blue-purple flowers. Grows 20–30 inches tall.	In sunny flower and herb gardens in spring.	For dried-flower crafts; hang upside down in bunches in a cool, dry spot.
Statice Plant bearing sprays of paperlike flowers in yellow, purple, blue, or rose. Grows 24 inches tall.	In gardens in summer; year-round at flower shops and craft stores in the dried-flower section. Dried stalks are more useful than fresh ones are.	For dried-flower crafts; pick flowers when fully open, then place them upright in a small amount of water and allow to dry.

Woodland Treasures

Forests are magical places, full of beautiful things to use in craft projects. If you look at the woods through the eyes of an artist, you will see a whole new world.

What	Where and When	How to Use
Artist's Fungus A beautiful striped, fan-shaped fungus that is gray or gray-brown, with a white underside. Grows 2–20 inches wide.	Grows on logs and stumps and is found year-round in the U.S., except in very southern regions, and in many parts of Canada. Buy at a craft store.	Great for all kinds of woodland crafts (see pages 28–32).
Burned Ground Moss Soft, velvety green tuft. Puts out spore cases (like small round flags) that are brown or purplish red. Grows about 1 inch tall.	Grows in fields, roadsides, and lawns throughout the year. Grows in almost all regions of the U.S. and many parts of Canada. Buy at a craft store.	This moss is great for a variety of woodland crafts (see pages 26–37, 40–53, 58–59, 67–69, 151–153, and 156).
Moss Soft ground cover.	Grows on the ground in almost all regions of the U.S. and many parts of Canada. Buy at a craft store. You may be able to buy bright green reindeer moss, too.	Great for all kinds of woodland crafts (see pages 26–37, 40–53, 58–59, 67–69, 151–153, and 156).
Cones Generally come from evergreen trees; made up of scales that fit together in an alternating pattern, like shingles on a roof. They vary in size from small to large, so choose what you need or use what you find. **Australian pine** trees love coastal and very warm regions. The cone is actually a fruit that looks like a cone. A great size for crafts. **Fir** are beautiful, graceful trees with large, rounded cones. Douglas fir has a three-pointed *bract*. **Hemlock** trees have short needles and upright cones found at the ends of the branches. **Lodgepole pine** is a very common tree in the West. Its cone is packed tightly at the base and slightly pointed at the top. **Shortleaf pine.** There are many, many kinds of pines, each with a slightly different cone. This one is rounded and grows on branches in twos or threes. **Spruce** trees grow mostly in northern regions. The cones are large and hang down from the branch. **Sweet gum ball** is a spiky ball that is not much good for crafts except as decoration.	Wherever evergreens grow (in most parts of the U.S. and Canada) you'll be able to find cones easily. 	Great for all kinds of woodland crafts (see pages 28–32, 34–37, 40–43, and 50–51.

Seeds and Beans

These are available from a wide range of sources — almost all plants produce seeds! You'll find seeds in the garden, in the woods, and at the supermarket. The following are just a few of the plants that offer useful seeds.

Cantaloupe
One of the muskmelons, cantaloupe has a hard, warty rind; sweet orange fruit; and many, many small seeds.

Cotton Boll
This is the seedpod for the cotton plant. After the seed forms, fibers begin to grow on the outside of the seed coat. They become squeezed into the pod until it bursts open, showing long, fluffy cotton.

Peach
The seed of the peach is called a pit or a stone. There are two kinds of peaches — the freestone, in which the pit separates easily from the fruit — and the clingstone, in which the pit really does cling to the fruit.

Sea Creatures

In coastal areas in North America, wherever the land meets the sea, there is abundant life. We go to the seashore not only to enjoy the ocean but also to walk along the beach and see the treasures that the ocean brings in. Each shore supports different types of shells and sea life. Use what you can find and what you like. The following are only a few of the many ocean jewels.

Clam (hard-shelled)
Abundant along the Atlantic Coast, clams are found in sand or mud near the low-tide mark.

Coquina
Sometimes these shells wash up on shore still attached, looking like the wings of a butterfly.

Murex
This is a heavy, ridged, spiny shell. The murex snail actually lives in deep ocean water, but the shell is often washed up on shore.

Mussel
You'll find these shells in cooler waters in sand or mud or attached to rocks by strong threads.

Sand Dollar
This is also called a sea biscuit and is a flat relative of the sea urchin. Once the animal dies, the skeleton often washes up on the beach and turns white as it is bleached by the sun.

Starfish
Each starfish has five to ten arms growing at sharp angles. If a starfish loses an arm, it will grow back.

Suggested Reading

Sometimes the best inspiration is to read stories about people who've already created some of the art represented in this book. This is a list of fiction and nonfiction books. Choose ones about crafts that particularly interest you.

Ahiagble, Gilbert. *Master Weaver from Ghana.* Greensboro, NC: Open Hand Publishing, 1989.

Baylor, Byrd. *When Clay Sings.* New York: Aladdin Paperbacks, 1987.

Cherkerzian, Diane. *Outdoor Fun: Great Things to Make and Do on Sunny Days.* Honesdale, PA: Boyds Mill Press, 1993.

Finley, Carol. *Art of the Far North: Inuit Sculpture, Drawing, and Printmaking.* Minneapolis: Lerner Publications Company, 1998.

Haab, Sherri. *Arts and Crafts Recipes.* New York: Klutz, 1998.

Hoyt-Goldsmith, Diane. *Totem Pole.* New York: Holiday House, 1990.

Kohl, MaryAnn F. *Good Earth Art: Environmental Art for Kids.* Bellingham, WA: Bright Ring Publishing, 1991.

La Pierre, Yvette. *Native American Rock Art: Messages from the Past.* West Palm Beach, FL: Lickle Publishing, 1994.

Larrabee, Lisa. *Grandmother Five Baskets.* Boulder, CO: Roberts Rinehart Publishers, 1993.

Lasky, Kathryn. *First Painter.* London: DK Publishing, 2000.

Lauber, Patricia. *Painters of the Cave.* Washington, DC: National Geographic Society, 1998.

Milord, Susan. *Adventures in Art: Art & Crafts Experiences for 8- to 13-Year-Olds.* Charlotte, VT: Williamson Publishing, 1997.

Musgrove, Margaret. *The Spider Weaver: A Legend of Kente Cloth.* New York: Blue Sky Press, 2001.

Newton Chocolate, Deborah M. *Kente Colors.* New York: Walker & Company, 1997.

Park, Linda Sue. *A Single Shard.* Boston: Clarion Books, 2001.

Perham, Molly. *North American Totem Poles: Secrets and Symbols of North America.* Toronto: Firefly Books, 1999.

Sullivan, Missy. *The Native American Look Book: Art and Activities from the Brooklyn Museum.* New York: The New Press, 1996.

Swentzell, Rina *Children of Clay: A Family of Pueblo Potters (We Are Still Here).* Minneapolis: Lerner Publications Company, 1992.

Gift Suggestions

When you finish a project, should you keep it or give it away? Art is a personal thing, and artists put a lot of themselves into the things they create. You may want to keep everything you make, but you also might want to bestow some as gifts to special people. If you do decide to make gifts, here are a few suggestions:

Index

Page numbers in **bold** indicate a project.
Page numbers in *italic* indicate a table or box.

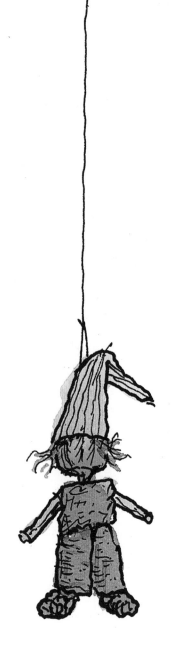